TRAVEL AND TRANSPORT IN IRELAND

TRAVEL
AND TRANSPORT
IN IRELAND

Edited by Kevin B. Nowlan

Gill & Macmillan

Published in Ireland by
Gill & Macmillan Ltd
Goldenbridge
Dublin 8
with associated companies throughout the world
© John G. Barry, Miriam Daly, Michael Herity,
Joseph Lee, Patrick Lynch, Oliver MacDonagh,
J. L. McCracken, W. A. McCutcheon, Kevin B. Nowlan,
Thomas P. O'Neill, Liam de Paor, Gerard Quinn 1973, 1993

0 7171 2118 6

Printed by Colour Books, Dublin

A catalogue record is available for this book from the
British Library.

Acknowledgements

Grateful acknowledgement is made to the following for assistance in selection of illustrations and for permission to reproduce pictures in this book: Pat Wallace; National Museum of Ireland; British Museum; RTE Reference Library; Linenhall Library, Belfast; National Library of Ireland; Ulster Museum; Ulster Folk Museum; Public Record Office, Northern Ireland; Ministry of Finance, Northern Ireland; County Museum, Armagh; *Illustrated London News;* Rex Roberts Studios; Derek Peyton; R. W. Hammond; Skyfotos Ltd; Harland & Wolff Ltd; Arthur Guinness Son & Co. Ltd; Bord Fáilte; CIE; Aer Lingus.

Publisher's Note

This edition of *Travel and Transport in Ireland* is a reprint of the hardback edition which first appeared in 1973. Apart from the correction of a few textual errors which appeared in the first impression, the text is unchanged.

The list of Contributors has, of course, been revised to take account of changes since 1973.

Contents

Contributors

MICHAEL HERITY
Associate Professor of Celtic Archaeology, University College, Dublin

LIAM DE PAOR
Formerly Lecturer in History, University College, Cork

THE LATE JOHN G. BARRY
Formerly Professor of Medieval History, University College, Cork

J. L. MCCRACKEN
Formerly Professor of History, New University of Ulster, Coleraine

W. A. MCCUTCHEON
Formerly Keeper of Technology, Ulster Museum, Belfast

THOMAS P. O'NEILL
Professor Emeritus of History, University College, Galway

KEVIN B. NOWLAN
Professor Emeritus of Modern History, University College, Dublin

JOSEPH LEE
Professor of Modern History, University College, Cork

OLIVER MACDONAGH
Professor of Modern History, Australian National University, Canberra

THE LATE MIRIAM DALY
  Formerly Lecturer in Economic History, Queen's University, Belfast

PATRICK LYNCH
  Professor Emeritus of Political Economy, University College, Dublin

GERARD QUINN
  Associate Professor of Political Economy, University College, Dublin

Introduction

THIS collection of essays had its origins in a series of Thomas Davis lectures broadcast by Radio Telefís Éireann in 1970. Since then, the individual authors have had the opportunity to revise and expand their contributions to make them more suitable for publication in book form.

This work makes no claim to be a comprehensive history of transport and communications in Ireland. It seeks, rather, to present the general reader with an impression of how succeeding generations sought to overcome geographical obstacles by improving internal lines of communication and by establishing links with other countries. Transport history has important implications not merely for the student of economic and social history but also for those concerned with political developments. Given our geographical position, it should be obvious how considerable a role communications have played in our history. In prehistoric times Ireland was firmly placed on the great Atlantic sea-coast route from southern Europe to the Scandinavian north. In Viking and later times the sea links were a major factor in helping to draw the Scottish isles and the northern and eastern seaboard of Ireland into close cultural, political and social contact. In the medieval and Tudor periods, however, the difficulties of travel to and within Ireland hindered the expansion and consolidation of English influences.

Though Ireland, with the possible exception of the north-eastern counties, was only marginally involved in the industrial revolution of the eighteenth and nineteenth centuries, the transport innovations of those times deeply influenced the pattern of life in Ireland. River navigations, canals and improved roads opened up the interior of the country in a way which earlier centuries had not known. The waterways made possible the easy and relatively cheap movement of grain, building materials and other bulk goods between inland places and the coast, while enterprises such as Bianconi's cars made travel more attractive and less expensive for many people. But it was the railways which brought the full benefits of the transport revolution to Ireland in the first half of the nineteenth century.

Despite the terrible trial of the Great Famine and financial and commercial difficulties, Ireland had, by the middle of the nineteenth century, an impressive network of railway lines operated by private enterprise. Indeed, one of the major sources of difficulty in the twentieth century, as the roads recovered their old ascendancy, was that Ireland was left with too elaborate a railway system in relation to the actual needs of a country where the short distance haul predominated.

The two world wars helped the railways economically but, in both North and South, the place of the railway in the structure of modern transport still remains a far from certain one. The return to the roads, with the advent of the internal combustion engine, marked the beginning of a new phase in the history of transport and it brought with it new problems: the financing of road construction; road safety; pollution of the atmosphere and a strengthening of the role of the major cities such as Dublin and Belfast as trading centres for ever larger hinterlands. But road transport also introduced a high measure of flexibility into commercial and private travel and the cross-channel car-ferries have increased still further the scope of bulk transport by road.

The establishment of Aer Lingus and associated companies marked a major capital investment by the community in air transport but the development of a national air service must be seen in its social context as well as in its strictly commercial one. The air services have helped to bring Ireland into closer contact than ever before with other countries. The process of breaking down what remains of the old isolation has been speeded up. For good or ill, changes in the means of transport continue to involve complex social, political and cultural consequences.

Kevin B. Nowlan

1 The Pre-historic Period: Internal and External Communications

Michael Herity

IF YOU take a cruise on one of the many pleasure-boats sailing down the Shannon river through Athlone these days, you will pass through a monument to Victorian technology, the lock just below the famous bridge where St Ruth held Ginkell in 1690. As you wait for the water-level to fall in the lock there will be plenty of time to read this inscription cut on the stone:

> Erected by the Commissioners for the Improvement of the
> Navigation of the River Shannon 1846
> Thomas Rhodes, Principal Engineer
> John Long, District Engineer
> Bernard Mullins, Contractor

It is particularly appropriate for a prehistorian to pay homage to the Shannon Commissioners and their servants, for it was these men, in their work of improving the Shannon navigation, who came upon great numbers of prehistoric implements of stone and of bronze which our prehistoric ancestors had dropped into the water at fording-places on this great river. These implements are important evidence upon which we can base suggestions about what routes were used by them and at which times these routes were used. We shall return to the Victorians and their finds in a moment; but first a word or two about how we must go about tracing the development of communications in the prehistoric period.

It is in the nature of things that the record of travel in prehistoric times will be pieced together more from the monuments and objects scattered along

V R
ERECTED BY THE COMMISSIONERS
FOR THE IMPROVEMENT OF THE NAVIGATION OF THE
RIVER SHANNON
1846
THO⁵ RHODES PRINCIPAL ENGINEER
JOHN LONG DISTRICT ENGINEER
BERNARD MULLINS CONTRACTOR

the ways by which people travelled than in the physical remains of roads, carts, horses and their trappings, or in boats and jetties. For most of the pre-historic period we cannot point to any extensive road system, to harbours or to the remains of boats. The great difficulties of discovering material which must have been deposited haphazardly, and which has also suffered 'the rude wasting of old time', not to speak of the problem of discovering what we would like to find, render any archaeological reconstruction like a jigsaw with a number of pieces missing.[1] For the most part then, we will be able to deduce indirectly that travel took place along the sea-routes and the riverways, that overland travellers may have sought out gravel ridges and the like where they could command a view of where they were bound for, and that bogs and woodlands were avoided. Where rivers were crossed, we owe it mainly to the Victorians that we know where the favoured crossing-points were located. In interpreting the evidence, we moderns must remember that ancient man had his own aspirations, not always as 'primitive' as we might think, and that his view of the potential of his environment was motivated by his needs as *he* saw them, not as *we* do.[2]

NEW STONE AGE: FROM 3000 B.C.

We should begin with the New Stone Age. Today, a dying community of folk tradition links the peoples all around the shores of Donegal Bay, from

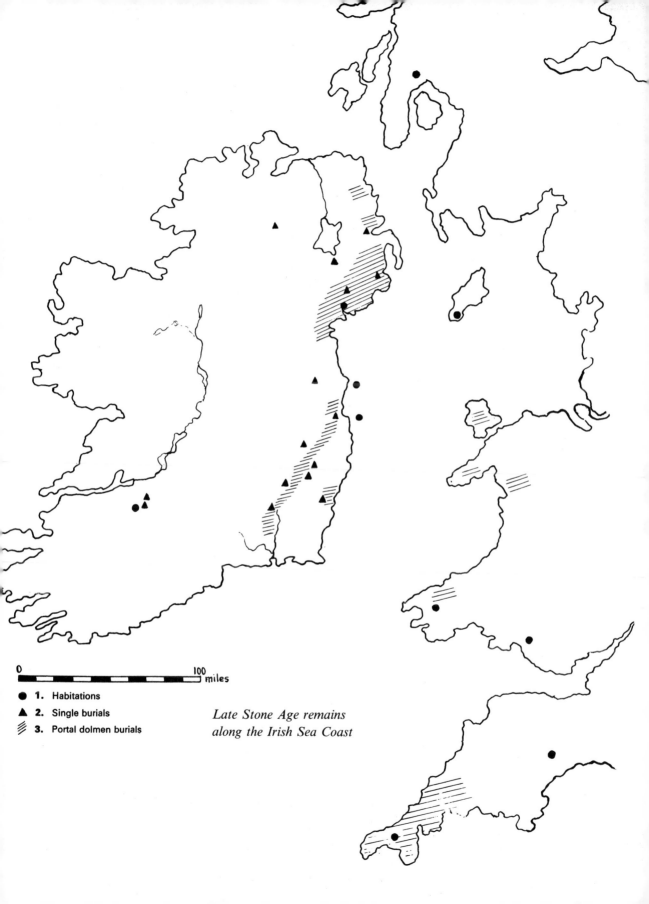

0   100
                                             miles

●   **1.** Habitations

▲   **2.** Single burials

▨   **3.** Portal dolmen burials

Late Stone Age remains
along the Irish Sea Coast

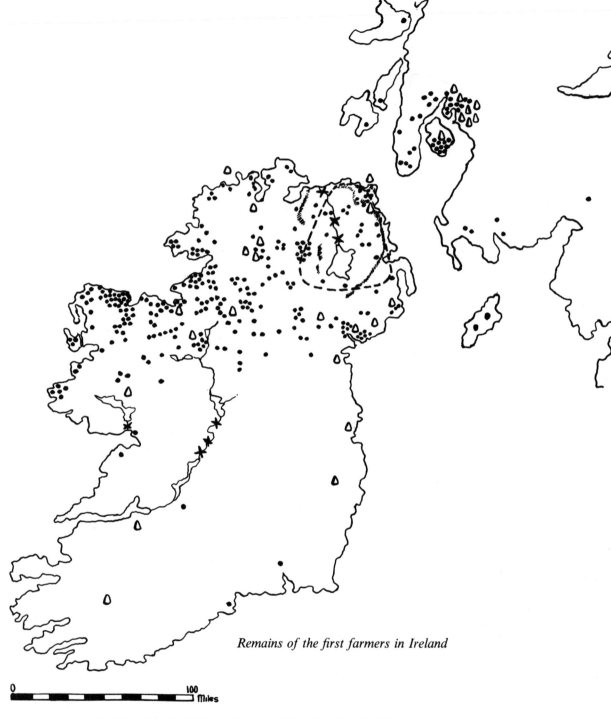

Remains of the first farmers in Ireland

0   100
Miles

●   **1.** Tombs: court cairns in Ireland and related tombs in west Scotland, after de Valera and Ó Nualláin, and Henshall

△   **2.** Find-places of axeheads of polished stone from Tievebulliagh, area of thickest distribution in the north-east shown within a broken line

✗   **3.** River crossing-points

⌇   **4.** Deposits of flint-bearing chalk in the north-east the Stags of Broadhaven eastward by the mouth of the Moy to Sligo town, and northward around Rosses Point and Bundoran to Killybegs and Glencolumbcille, indicating that coastal routes now dead were until recently the easiest means of communication between the peoples living on the shores of this great semicircle. About 3000 B.C., at the beginning of the New Stone Age, this area was the earliest chosen to be colonised by the first farmers who arrived here from the Atlantic coast of France. It continued to be favoured by them for at least a thousand years, during which time they built up a system of farming that enabled them to devote their surplus wealth to the building of magnificent stone tombs called court cairns which are found at their finest around the shores of Donegal Bay, at places like Malin More in Donegal, Creevykeel in Sligo and Ballyglass in Mayo.[3] These farmers brought with them cereals from France and set these in stone-fenced fields but they must soon have learnt that it was in cattle that the great wealth of Ireland lay. These cattle must also have been brought hog-tied in their boats from Atlantic Europe, for no wild cattle have been found in Ireland from the time before the coming of these first farmers.[4]

The use of metals was not known to these folk, who relied on stone tools to help in the clearance of land for cultivation and possibly even for tillage. So they fashioned tools of polished stone from the most suitable rocks to be found, and the mountainside of Tievebulliagh in Co. Antrim, the source of

PLAN AND DIAGRAM SECTION OF TOOME BAR, LOUGH NEAGH

Bunatrahir Bay near Ballycastle on the north coast of Mayo. The heaviest concentration of the court cairns of the first farmers is found immediately round this bay. It appears to have been the first landfall of these farmers in Ireland.

6

supply of a suitable rock, porcellanite, became our first industrial site.⁵
Nature had seen to it that flint, the very hard stone prized by these people for
making their penknives, arrowheads and other tools, was to be found only
in this north-eastern area, in a narrow deposit of chalk running through the
counties of Antrim and Derry and Down. No wonder the *entrepreneurs* of the
Stone Age settled extensively here in the north east, where the industrial
wealth of Stone Age Ireland was to be found.

RIVER CROSSINGS

A network of routes quickly grew up between west and east Ulster,
marked by the tombs of these small-farming folk, and also marked at three
crossing-points of the Bann river, Portglenone, Portna Shoal and Toome
Bar, where the operations of the Board of Works had recovered several stone
axeheads by the middle of the last century. Fords formed at eskers across the
bed of the Shannon were discovered at the same time in the operations of the
Shannon Commissioners, when the bed of the river was lowered by a depth
of six feet at Keelogue, south of Banagher, and several stone axeheads and
bronze implements were found. In fact half of the Royal Irish Academy's
collection of polished stone axeheads in 1857 consisted of Shannon implements. Griffiths, the Chief Commissioner, was inclined to interpret these as
the remains of battles between Leinster and Connaught men, but it is more
likely that they represent the losses of traders or ordinary folk at this perilous
point on a journey from one province into another.⁶ The esker which had
to be removed from the river bed at Keelogue was obviously part of a great
esker highway linking Leinster and Connaught.

By making a map of all Tievebulliagh stone axeheads that have been found,
we can get an idea of its importance as an industrial site. These are found in
great numbers in Antrim, of course, but have also been found as far away as
Kent in the south of England.

PASSAGE GRAVE BUILDERS

While it might be said that these first travellers got here by accident, not
knowing the arts of ocean navigation, the Passage Grave builders, who sailed
up the Irish Sea to the Boyne mouth about five hundred years later, appear
to have been in full control of their destiny. It was these highly sophisticated
people who built the magnificent Boyne Valley tombs now being excavated—

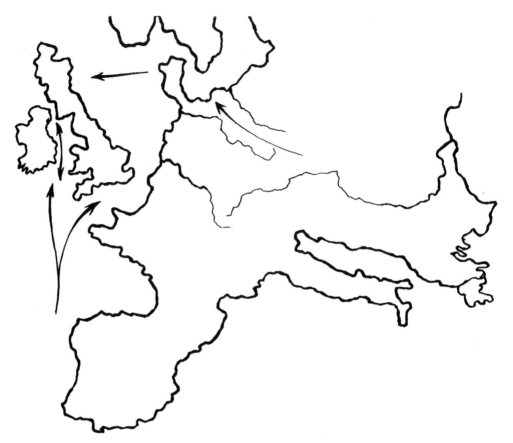

Ireland's contacts with the Atlantic and with Central Europe, 2000 B. C.

it has been suggested that one carving at New Grange is a representation of one of their ships—and who set up our first links across the Irish Sea in Anglesey and Pembrokeshire.[7] Inland they set up large cemeteries at Lough Crew near Oldcastle, Carrowkeel west of the Curlews near Boyle, and Carrowmore near Sligo town, as well as extending south into Wicklow and north into the flint area of Antrim, Derry and Down, where their tombs cluster in great numbers. Whereas their continental ancestors had sited their tombs on rises in the ground, in Ireland these people sought out mountain tops for their tombs as at Knocknarea, Co. Sligo, Slieve Gullion in Armagh, Seefin and Seehan on the borders of Dublin and Wicklow, and, highest of all, Slieve Donard in Co. Down, almost 3,000 feet up. Perhaps the inter-visibility achieved by this seeking for heights had a functional motivation in that it gave a bird's eye view of the countryside. A granite boulder transported all the way from the Mourne Mountains was used to make a stone basin at New Grange.

The climate of Ireland at this early period was warmer and drier than it is now, resembling that of the latitude of Paris at the present day.[8] Forests which grew freely on the now windy and barren west coast can still be seen under blanket bogs which began to grow on the hillslopes of the west in a period of worsening climate which set in during the millennium beginning at 2000 B.C. Many of the tombs, fields and farmsteads of the Stone Age communities can now be seen buried in this peat, like ruined cities buried under desert sands.[9] Adaptations in shelter and modes of travel followed this change, while a search for new pastures must have been progressively forced on the farmers of the areas engulfed in bogland.

THE IRISH SEA AND CENTRAL EUROPE—2000 B.C.

At 2000 B.C. a new polarisation can be seen in the direction of travel, which up to this time had tended to run east-west.[10] The Irish Sea now became a route uniting Cornwall and Argyll 350 miles apart with ports at Waterford, Pembrokeshire, Dublin, Anglesey, Carlingford, the Isle of Man, Galloway and the Mull of Kintyre. The islands of Dalkey and Lambay off the Dublin coast came into prominence as staging-posts on this great route. The reason for this change appears to have been the discovery of newly-important mineral deposits of copper, gold and tin in Wicklow, Waterford and Cornwall by prospectors coming across Scandinavia and Scotland from the great centres of metallurgy in Central Europe. Travel by the Rhine and Elbe brought these adventurers into the North Sea, where Jutland's amber wealth may have been the primary attraction, and tales of the Atlantic *El Dorado* attracted them into the Irish Sea. New burial modes, new kinds of pottery, and new implements, ornaments and ornamental motifs in the new metals are now found in this Irish Sea Zone. Reaching Ireland by this route in pre-historic times required more than mere everyday effort even with the benefit of water travel; a fair parallel is Buck Whaley's two years to Jerusalem and back in the eighteenth century A.D.

Ireland's position out in the Atlantic might have left her an *Ultima Thule* clinging in isolation to the old Atlantic Stone Age ways. Despite her amber wealth, Jutland, much closer to the new centres of metallurgy down the Elbe, achieved the status of a free port more than that of manufacturing centre at this stage, while more remote Ireland showed direct contact with central European metallurgy. At 2000 B.C. Ireland stands at the north-west apex of a great triangle of routes joining Transylvania to the south east, Huelva in Iberia and the southern end of the Irish Sea. No doubt it was the gold of Croghan Kinshela south of Avoca in Co. Wicklow that was responsible for Ireland's importance all through the Bronze Age despite the difficulties of reaching this country, and it was our gold which attracted not only prospectors and miners into Ireland, but also continental craftsmen whose insular pupils brought about some spectacular innovations in ornamental styles. The distribution of one Irish gold ornament of the Early Bronze Age, the lunula, gives an idea of how widespread contacts were at that period; by far the greatest number of these are found in Ireland, with a few examples in Denmark, Belgium, North Germany, Cornwall and on the Atlantic and northern coasts of France, while a poorer analogue, the jet necklace, is found mainly in Scotland[11].

WHEELED VEHICLES AND TRACKWAYS

While small traders and prospectors had little need of more than a horse to carry their gear overland like the travelling packmen of the last century, a wider scale of operations is intimated by the appearance of wheeled vehicles in northern Europe about 2000 B.C.[12] The ultimate source of these lies far away to the south east on the flat lands of Transcaucasia between the Black Sea and the Caspian where carts with two or sometimes four wheels are found as early as 2500 B.C. in pit graves under burial mounds. The wheels of these were disc-wheels of solid wood, of a kind which were in use in Ireland on country carts up to recent times. (Thomas Dinely illustrates a two-wheeled cart called a Rings-End Coach fitted with disc-wheels which was used for taking passengers from the cross-channel boats near the Pigeon House to the centre of Dublin in the seventeenth century.[13]) Examples of these wooden disc-wheels have been found in Germany, the Netherlands and Denmark; in one case in the Netherlands, at Nieuwe Dordrecht, one was found beside a wooden trackway.[14] It appears from this evidence that the introduction of disc-wheeled carts into the relatively rougher and damper terrain of northern

Europe required the invention of roadbuilding about 2000 B.C. Other evidence of the cultural background would link these people with the diaspora of Indo-European linguistic groups.

Trackways of this early date, or possibly of an even earlier date, have long been known from the Somerset Levels, south of the Mendip Hills near Bristol, where recent investigation has shown them extending up to 600 yards in length.[15] Several trackways of this kind are known in Ireland but few can be securely dated as early as 2000 B. C. One which appears to be early was found at a depth of seven feet in Ballykillen Bog near Edenderry, Co. Offaly in the last century.[16] We know little enough about its features but two finds associated with it give a clear indication of a date in the Early Bronze Age, not long after 2000 B. C. One of these is an antler axehead eight inches long of a type known in northern Europe from much earlier times; the second is a rare find, a neatly-formed tanged arrowhead of flint tied into the head of its briarwood shaft with a piece of gut. It can now be seen with the Murray Collection in the museum of Cambridge University. The arrowhead appears to be an Early Bronze Age type, so it seems fair to date the Ballykillen trackway to the

Wooden trackway in a bog at Corlona, Co. Leitrim, c. 1600 B.C. (after Tohall)

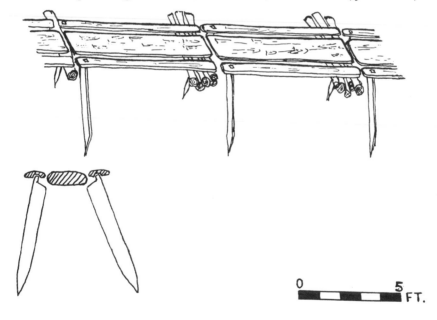

II

period shortly after 2000 B. C. and to deduce that it was built to take disc-wheeled vehicles whose ancestry lay far to the south-east on the plains of the Near East.

We have a much better record of an early trackway discovered to science less than twenty years ago at Corlona Bog in Co. Leitrim.[17] Here a section, a kilometre (say, five-eighths of a mile) in length was surveyed running in a straight line in a south-easterly direction into Ardlougher townland, where a paved pathway running on the firm ground at the edge of the bog may have continued the line of the trackway. It was built in sections about seven or eight feet long, each section consisting of a main plank flanked on either side by a narrower outer plank, making the track about three feet in width. Stout piles driven obliquely five feet deep into the bog supported both the main and the outer beams at their west end, the east end being laid on a pile of loose branches laid at right angles to the line of the trackway, presumably to cushion the passing of the load from one section of trackway to the next, possibly from east to west. The narrowness of this roadway seems to rule out its use by wheeled vehicles, but examination of the wear on the joins of an unexposed portion might provide better evidence.

A botanical examination of the bog in which this trackway ran suggested that it was built at a period of increasing rainfall; this was dated roughly to 1500 B.C. by means of a radiocarbon determination. It was about this time that many of the bogs in Ireland began to flourish, necessitating radical adjustments in the way of life of the people. The excellent carpentry of the trackway indicates the use of bronze tools by skilled tradesmen for the making of long planks of even width and thickness and for the making of mortice-and-tenon joins between the supporting piles and the planks of the trackway itself.

In describing these trackways I have implied that their building had a purely functional motivation. There are those, however, who would interpret at least some of these structures as having to do with ritual. This suggestion finds some confirmation in the discovery of a wooden hermaphrodite figure, crude but unmistakeable, directly under the Bell track in Somerset. Possibly their occurrence can be connected with cults like the one indicated by the 'sun-chariot' of somewhat later date found at Trundholm in Denmark.[18]

One of the luxuries imported from a great distance about the time of the building of the Corlona trackway was segmented beads of blue faience, a kind of glazed paste made in the east Mediterranean. Several have been found in Ireland and south Britain, and a necklace of segmented faience beads with beads of copper and amber came up at the excavations at Tara.[19] No doubt these were traded for Irish gold and copper.

If Ireland's relations with the Continent in this period are polarised along the Atlantic seaways and a North Sea axis, her cultural and trading relationships with Britain are similarly divided: either they are with a northern province extending as far south as the river Ouse or with a southern province centred on the area known to prehistorians as Wessex.[20] Beaker and Food Vessel pottery found with single burials of the Early Bronze Age show clear evidence of this duality,[21] while a similar north-south polarisation is clear from the trade in daggers and goldwork from Wessex to Ireland although Irish gold lunulae and halberds are absent from this southern province.[22] Meanwhile Cornwall continues to be a staging-post on the Atlantic route to Europe.

LATER BRONZE AGE—1000 B.C.

By 1000 B.C. or so, when wet conditions prevailed and a climate rather like today's had appeared, serious accommodations were made necessary. Bronze technology had now improved tremendously; smiths' and merchants' hoards were much larger than ever before; new kinds of tools and weapons were produced, and new techniques for making them had evolved.[23] A more vigorous mining campaign must have been undertaken to support this expanding industry in the coppermines to the south east in Kerry, Cork and Tipperary. Continued goldmining provided the raw material for new fashions in ornament, and the seaways were busier than ever before.

Despite the excellent preservative powers of the bogs, virtually no habitations or farmsteads are known in the period 1200 B.C. to 500 B.C. which would give a picture of the farming base which supported and provided patronage for the extensive industry in metals.[24] But the implements of war, heavy slashing swords and rounded shields, are found in great numbers from the period about 700 B.C. A family of gold ornaments dating from about the same time clustered around the Shannon estuary[25]—many of them found in the eighteenth century in the famous Golden Bog of Cullen near Tipperary town[26]—are akin to ornaments of the same period found in the Nordic Zone, Scandinavia and North Germany. Amber from that zone formed

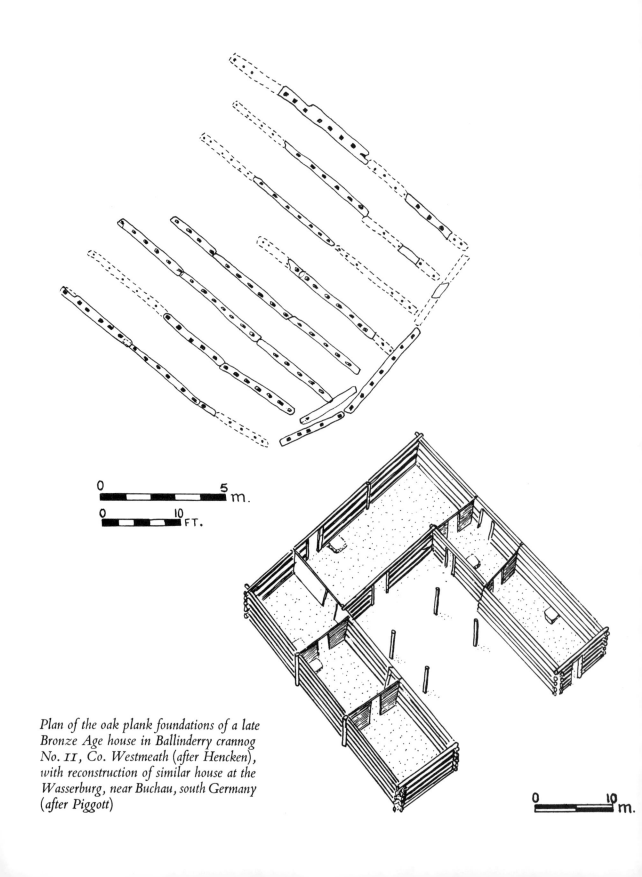

0   5 m.

0   10 FT.

*Plan of the oak plank foundations of a late
Bronze Age house in Ballinderry crannog
No. II, Co. Westmeath (after Hencken),
with reconstruction of similar house at the
Wasserburg, near Buchau, south Germany
(after Piggott)*

0   10 m.

massive necklaces, like one of 300 beads found near the remains of an ancient trackway at Whitegates near Kells, Co. Meath,[27] and suggests a reciprocal trade across the North Sea.

The crannog, a new more formalised lake-dwelling, was introduced towards the end of the Bronze Age. Normally circular, these crannogs were surrounded by rows of piles driven into the lake-bed within which a radial arrangement of logs covered with layers of brushwood and stones raised the level of the dwellings out of the water. These are a gift to archaeologists, since the water preserves an almost complete range of material from the time of their building and use. The earliest of these are found at Knocknalappa, Co. Clare and Ballinderry, Co. Offaly; this Ballinderry lake-dwelling has a large aisled house covering an area of 150 square metres and built of large upright posts set in solid beams laid in the ground. In form it appears to be related to structures found down the Rhine in Germany in lake-dwellings of similar form like the famous Wasserburg near Buchau.[28]

Jetties have been found built to one side of these crannogs, and dug-out boats are frequently found in the lake beds. It may be that a time of unrest stimulated the people to adopt this obviously defensive dwelling, despite the discomfort of living at a distance from their farms on the mainland. A cheek-piece of red deer antler, part of a horse's head-piece found at the Ballinderry site, suggests that the horse was used at least as a pack-animal. Other metal objects suggest parade. Several corduroy roads of this period are known from all over the country; a typical one of these found at Ballyalbanagh, Co. Antrim, was seven feet wide and formed of longitudinal oak beams sheeted with transverse oak planking.[29] Its width suggests provision for cart or wagon transport.

The Celts and The Earliest Maps

About 300 B.C. when the art of iron-working was borne into Ireland by Celtic groups stemming originally from the valley of the Upper Danube, little change was made in this aspect of life. Bronze continued to be used for prestige objects, while iron-working became a backyard industry giving superior everyday tools and weapons. The Celtic mythology so abundantly preserved in Ireland indicates the extensive use of horse and chariot for personal transport. Ornamental bronze horse-bits are commonly found, and the corduroy roads continued to be built, though the chariot burials of the

15

La Tène facet of the Iron Age found abundantly in eastern France and in Yorkshire have not yet been found in Ireland.

We are fortunate in being able to reconstruct from historical sources a map made by Ptolemy of Alexandria, one of a number of famous classical geographers, about 200 A.D.[30] He shows a good knowledge of the capes and rivers of Ireland, and also of the names of the various tribes living throughout the country. Here is a much more direct source from which to gauge the scope of travel and trading around the coasts of Ireland in the Late Bronze Age and Early Iron Age.

Caesar arrived in Britain in the middle of the first century B.C. The military sense and highly organised system of provincial government of the Romans led to the building there of a network of dead straight highways like Watling Street in England and the Via Appia in Italy itself. The five great roads which history tells us radiated from Tara may have been modelled on these. A few stretches of straight durable road can be seen at what are recognised in our mythology and early history as Celtic royal sites, three lengths up to 100 yards long at Maeve's site of Cruachain in Co. Roscommon,[31] and a shorter length which is the alleged Banqueting Hall at Tara. But these appear more like ceremonial ways than everyday roads.

THE BROIGHTER BOAT

A gold model of a boat, found with a gold neck-torc of Celtic design at Broighter near Derry a little before 1900[32] helps give us an idea of what other sea-going vessels of the period were like. Nine thwarts provided seating for a crew to work eighteen oars, two to each oar. A mast stepped through the central thwart and provided with a yard and three booms may have been rigged with mainsail and topsail, as well as jib and spinnaker. Steering was by an oar fitted on the starboard side of the stern.

Caches of Roman silver belonging to the first few centuries A.D. are the material result of Irish piracy on the west coast of Britain.[33] More may have been taken away than mere silver: new kinds of ornament to be imitated and adapted, a Roman engineer who would later supervise a road-building programme, or the slaves whose iron shackles have been found at Ardakillen near Strokestown and the royal lake-dwelling of Lagore in Co. Meath.[34]

Easily the most important of these slaves was called Cutric by the Irish and Patrick by his own people. When he came back to Ireland in 432, Christianity and literacy began and the prehistoric period was at an end.

If Patrick arrived as a slave on the east coast, it was from a port on the Atlantic that he took a boat for Europe. At 432, things focus once more on western and Atlantic Europe.

Broighter Boat

2 The Early Historic Period: Monks and Traders

Liam de Paor

THE first traveller in Ireland who has left us any account of his journeyings is St Patrick. From him we learn that he first came to Ireland as a captive, taken in one of the Irish raids on Britain which marked the declining years of the western Roman empire in that province, and that when a voice heard in his sleep urged him to escape and return to his home, he made a journey of 200 miles across Ireland to the ship which would take him away from Irish shores. In his account of his mission to the Irish, he refers in several passages to his travels about the country with a retinue which included the sons of kings, and he tells us that he has preached the Gospel 'unto those parts beyond which there lives nobody'. We learn little from St Patrick, however, about the means or conditions of travel except that these could be hazardous, for him at least. More than once he was in danger of his life, more than once taken captive, and for one period of a fortnight he was held in chains.

From the following centuries there is a good deal of evidence of various kinds, and we can piece together some idea of what Irish travel was like in the 700 years from the coming of St Patrick until the coming of Strongbow. In the course of so long a passage of time naturally there were changes, but most of these do not seem to have been radical, and we can make some general statements about travel and transport for the period as a whole.

To begin with, hazards and difficulties were always there just as they were in St Patrick's time. There were several reasons for this. The country was much more thinly populated than at present; a total population for the whole island of less than half a million would be a good guess for the twelfth century when the Norman invasion took place, and there were probably far fewer people here at the time of St Patrick's mission in the fifth century. Population was unevenly distributed, with many uninhabited or sparsely inhabited tracts of mountain, forest and bog. In such conditions the traveller was exposed to dangers, to some extent perhaps from wild beasts, but to a much greater extent from wild men—outlaws and robbers—who waited in the wilderness beyond the settled lands. Numerous passing references in the literature testify to the prevalence of this menace to the traveller. Other hazards arose from the primitive condition of roads and tracks, especially where rivers or mountains were to be crossed, and again we have many stories and references which illustrate the difficulties and dangers of negotiating rough ways.

Another difficulty or hazard arose, not so much from the physical conditions of the time as from the social and legal system of early Ireland. For most of the period we are concerned with, Ireland was not in any sense politically centralised, but consisted politically of a large number—probably well over a hundred—of small more or less autonomous units. Such a unit was called a *tuath,* and at its head and representing it in dealings with the outside world was a *rí* or king. Within the *tuath,* society was stratified in grades from the king and his kinsmen at the top to the slaves at the bottom. For those at the lower end of the scale there was little prospect of travelling from their own place except in very unusual circumstances: they were bound by their servitude or by their work. Even for those at the upper end of the scale, travelling was not easy, for a man's status and protection depended chiefly upon his kin-group, which would exact satisfaction for any injury done to him and which was liable for any injury he might do. The operation of such a system of legal sanctions depended on the presence of the kin-group, and therefore it could only work effectively within the *tuath.* The man who took it into his head to travel from Kerry to Donegal was for practical purposes almost without protection. Journeys of this kind therefore would not be lightly undertaken.

However, there were important exceptions. One grade in the social system, known as the *Aes dána,* included people whose status derived from their skill in poetry, learning or craftsmanship. These could and did travel freely, protected by custom and by the local rulers. In Christian times the clergy came to share this special status, and in the course of time Irish monks became a byword for wandering, not only in their own country, but also overseas. The travels of poets, monks and craftsmen to and from one end of Ireland to the other ensured that the country, which never achieved effective political unity, was from a very early period culturally unified. As far back as we can trace Irish literature Ireland was, in a full sense, a nation (although not a nation-state); this can be attributed to the freedom of travel of those who had in their keeping the faith, values and higher culture of the people.

Although in early times most kings of *tuatha* acknowledged over-kings and most of these in turn acknowledged the suzerainty of one or other of the provincial kings, these subordinations were essentially external relations. That is to say, the subordinate king paid a tribute, while the over-king made a payment in return which was known as *tuarastal* but he did not concern himself with the internal affairs of the tributary *tuath*. Towards the end of our period, however, there are many indications that this had changed and that many of the more powerful provincial kings were trying at least to govern in some sense the whole of the provinces under their control, and were taking rulers such as Charlemagne or Alfred as their models. One of the marks of the good king, on this new kind of model, was that he could ensure safety of travel throughout a wide realm. So we find a twelfth-century eulogist of Brian Bóroimhe demonstrating Brian's qualities as a king by telling how a woman, alone, wearing her best jewellery, could travel freely and unmolested across Ireland in his time, the same hypothetical lady who took Thomas Moore's fancy when he wrote 'Rich and rare were the gems she wore'.

What were the means of travel in those times? It is plain that a great many people moved on foot; this, indeed, was probably the commonest way of getting about but there is not much to be said about it. Walking is walking: it requires only the simplest of trails and the prospect of some kind of shelter at intervals of ten or fifteen miles. There were no towns as we understand them in pre-Viking Ireland although the major monastic establishments would have resembled large villages, only parts of which were devoted to purely ecclesiastical purposes. The monasteries recognised a duty of providing hospitality for the wayfarer. Monasteries were numerous and one of their functions clearly was to serve as the inns or hotels of their time. Many of the larger ones must have derived a considerable revenue from pilgrims, and some indulged in what it would not be too much of an exaggeration to call tourist promotion. Read this description of Kildare from the Life of Brigid written in the seventh century by Cogitosus:

WHAT ELOQUENCE could sufficiently extol the beauty of this church and the innumerable wonders of what we may call its city. For city is the proper word to use. Kildare earns the title because of the multitudes who live there: it is a great metropolitan city. Within its outskirts, whose limits were laid out by St Brigid no man need fear any mortal adversary or any gathering of enemies; it is the safest refuge among all the enclosed towns of the Irish, with all their fugitives. The wealth and treasures of kings are in secure safe-keeping there, and the city is known to have reached the highest peak of good order. And who could number the varieties of people who gather there in countless numbers from all provinces? Some come for the abundance of the feasts, others, in ill-health, come for a cure, others come simply to watch the crowds go by, others come with great offerings to take part in the celebrations of the feast of St Brigid, who fell asleep on the Kalends of February and, laying aside quietly the burden of her flesh, followed by the Lamb of God into the heavenly mansions.

Most of the crowds mentioned here would have travelled on foot, as would most of those coming to the secular Aonach, held periodically at one assembly place or another. The Irish had horses, of course, and they rode them at times, but there does not seem to be much evidence to suggest that it was usual to make journeys of any length on horseback. On the contrary most important or well-to-do people, as almost every casual reference in the literature would indicate, travelled in horsedrawn wheeled vehicles.

This raises an interesting question, for travel by wheeled vehicles is possible only if there is some system of roads. We know that there was in fact a road system in early Ireland. The laws deal with it, and the various kinds of roads and tracks are mentioned from time to time in other literature. Different words are used for different kinds of roads—*slige, rámut, sét, rót, bóthar.* The *slige* was an important or main road for the use of wheeled vehicles, and the five great roads which are said to have radiated out from Tara bear this name—*Slighe Cualann, Slighe Midluachra,* and so on. There was a general legal obligation on the people through whose territories it passed to keep a public road free of 'brushwood, of water and of weeds'. The people of the *tuath* were similarly required to keep clean the *rámut*, that is the avenue leading to the fort of the king of the *tuath*. The word 'bóthar', which of course is the

21

Wooden trackway dating from the Viking period recently excavated at High Street in Dublin

usual modern Irish word for a road, meant originally, as its form would indicate, a cattleway. What are often called 'sunken ways' are known to archaeologists overseas in Celtic contexts, and similar sunken ways of uncertain date have been identified here—one, for example on the Curragh of Kildare. Such tracks for cattle going to pasture would probably not have been passable for wheeled vehicles, being too miry. The description that *Cormac's Glossary* gives of the bóthar sufficiently indicates its purpose: 'Two cows fit upon it, one lengthways, the other sideways, their calves and yearlings with them'. The motorist who has ever come upon a herd at milking time in his road will recognise the situation envisaged by the glossator.

We have little so-far-identified material evidence of the ancient roads. Some old roads and tracks can be traced on maps or on air photographs, but dating is extremely difficult. From time to time lengths of corduroy road, that is timber road or track, with logs laid transversely and pegged down, have been found in bogs. Again dating is difficult, but Mr Breandán Ó Riordáin of the National Museum in his excavations at High Street in Dublin has revealed somewhat similar wooden paths and ways, the streets of the Viking city.

The vehicle for which the main roads catered is called an Irish *carbat*, in Latin *currus*, and in English usually by the incorrigibly romantic word 'chariot'. It is a type of vehicle which had a very long history before it was used in Ireland, and it is well known from both literary and archaeological evidence among the Continental Celts. It was used by the Celts, as by other and earlier ancient peoples, in warfare but not it would seem as a kind of tank thundering through the enemy ranks; rather as a kind of taxi, carrying the warrior to his chosen position on the battlefield. It is thus that the chariot appears in the Irish saga-literature, especially the *Táin*. In the literature of the historic period, the chariot is essentially a means of transport, normally on peaceful occasions. Professor David Greene has recently made a study of the chariot of the Irish texts, and on the basis of the descriptions, references and technical terms in these, has constructed a vehicle which is essentially the same as we see depicted in relief on the high crosses of the eighth, ninth and tenth centuries. This is a two-wheeled cart drawn by a pair of small horses or ponies. A pole ran between the two, with a double wooden yoke near its tip which rested on their necks. The body of the vehicle was a low-sided flat framework, riding high above the axle, and probably long and narrow in proportion. The driver or charioteer apparently sat in front, perhaps with his

23

feet resting on the pole, and his passenger sat behind. The whole thing would look quite like the traditional Irish type of farm cart well known to most of us, except that instead of a pair of shafts for one pony, there was a centre-pole for two. The wheels were spoked and were banded or tyred with iron, indicating quite a high degree of sophistication and skill in woodworking. But archaeology has by now produced quite an impressive amount of evidence for the skill in carpentry of the early Irish.

It seems that the chariot was normally dismantled when not in use, the wheels being taken off. A story told by Adomnán in his Life of Columba bears on this:

AT ANOTHER TIME, when the saint was living for some days in Ireland, compelled by ecclesiastical affairs he entered a chariot that had previously been blessed by him, and that had been yoked, but by some unknown negligence without the necessary bolts having first been inserted through the holes in the ends of the axle-tree. It was Colmán, Echuid's son, a holy man, the founder of the monastery that is called in the Irish language Snám luthir, who on that day acted as driver in the chariot of St Columba. The day's driving over the long distances they travelled did not cause any separation of the wheels from the axle-shoulders, or any slackening, although, as has been said above, the wheels were held on by no retaining or securing bolts; God's grace alone so preserving the venerable man that the chariot in which he sat followed a true course, safely and without any hindrance.

Even when the linch-pins were not omitted, it seems from many other stories that the chariot was all too liable to lose or damage a wheel in travelling over rough stony roads. It must in any case have been a slow means of travelling since it seems probable that the number of what could be called highways was small. It seems also that, at least before the eleventh century, there were few if any bridges of any size in the country. Rivers were normally crossed at fords, and this means that by land as well as by water, travel would have been extremely difficult in the winter half of the year. In the century or so immediately before the Norman invasion, we do find occasional references to bridges, such as one which Tairdelbach O'Brien is said to have built across the Shannon at Killaloe in 1071. It is not clear, however, what kind of bridges these were; whether a true bridge was built, under which the water flowed, or whether a kind of timber causeway was made, through which the river passed. At any rate the eleventh and twelfth centuries appear to have been a period in which in the communications system as in many other aspects of life, progressive changes were being made.

We hear little of the transport of goods and commodities within Ireland, or indeed of trade of any kind within the country. It is difficult to know how far the elaborate system of tribute and *tuarasdal* operated in practice, and how far the exchange of commodities (as well as cattle) envisaged in it was more than nominal. But Irish society was predominantly pastoral: the cows provided much of the food and drink and also contributed to clothing the people. Crops were sown too, to supplement the diet of dairy produce with bread, porridge and beer, and a very high degree of self-sufficiency—almost complete so far as the necessities of life were concerned—must have been reached by most rural communities. There must have been some movement of salt. The reduction of iron from bog-ores was extremely widespread, according to the evidence provided by the archaeological excavation of habitation sites, and iron knives and other necessary or useful implements were also a widespread local manufacture. Evidence of bronze-working—the manufacture of pins and other small objects of utility and ornament—has been found in many parts of the country. Again a measure of self-sufficiency is indicated, although there were probably travelling smiths who stayed in a locality long enough to supply its needs for a fairly long period, and then moved on elsewhere. There were probably also travelling stonemasons and carvers who perhaps made querns and millstones as well as churches and other stone buildings. In fact stone for building or for carving is one commodity which must have been transported for some distance, since suitable stone for masons' purposes was not available in every district. But trade in general was not a feature of pre-Viking Ireland, and even after the Viking invasions it was not until the end of the tenth century that the first coins were minted in the country and not until long after that again that they began to affect, as currency, the Irish outside the Norse towns.

While there is thus little evidence for any internal trade, the country was not wholly self-sufficient. From very early times some external trade had been conducted. There are indications that the wine trade was in progress before

This currach, photographed at the end of the last century, is probably very similar to the primitive craft of early times

the advent of Christianity, and a scatter of finds of Roman coins and other objects would seem to indicate that there were contacts—not always in the form of hostile raids—with the Roman Empire long before the time of St Patrick. The Celtic peoples in general had long enjoyed a reputation in the Mediterranean world as customers for wine, and it seems that the Irish were no exception to this. Christianity would have swelled the demand for wine, since it was now needed for the altar, and would also have stimulated some demand for oil. The trade is documented in two ways: in finds of pottery, at coastal sites especially, which demonstrate that in the centuries immediately after St Patrick's time, Ireland was maintaining contact by way of the wine trade with western France and beyond it the Mediterranean; and in references to the trade in Continental sources from which we know, for example, that Merovingian wine ships plied to Clonmacnoise. At a later period we have archaeological evidence for trade across the Irish Sea, and in the twelfth century Giraldus Cambrensis tells us that there was a brisk traffic between Bristol and the eastern parts of Ireland. He informs us further, and we know also from other sources, that one of the Irish imports of this period was slaves.

We are brought here to the question of travel and transport by water, always of very great importance in early times. Ireland is not only an island with an indented, and therefore long coastline, but it is an island where most of the drainage is to the interior, producing many lakes and long rivers. As a result travel by water appears almost as frequently in our early records as travel by land. The people in most parts of the country were familiar with boats, and some of the monks, especially those of the monasteries of St Columba who had established his main centre on the little island of Iona off the western Scottish coast, appear to have spent a great part of their lives coming and going by water.

Almost certainly the commonest kind of craft on Irish waters, whether fresh or salt, was the *coracle* or *currach* or *naomhóg,* or some variant on these. This is the ancient boat-type of the Atlantic seaboard of Europe, still surviving in the Eskimo *umiak* and in the canvas-covered canoes of our west coast. This type of vessel has a light framework of wood, over which in early times not canvas but skins sewn together were stretched. Nor were the early coracles all small vessels like the canoes of present-day Connemara fishermen. It seems that some of them were quite large and perhaps had sails, although in one of the earliest references we have to the Irish seafarers, a passage in the Latin poet

27

A model of the type of ship in which St Brendan the Navigator sailed

Claudian referring to Irish raids on Roman Britain at the end of the fourth century, we are told that 'the sea foamed with hostile oars'. It is probably in such a vessel that St Patrick was carried into slavery in Ireland.

We do know however that other, heavier kinds of vessel were built. The Life of St Brendan the Navigator has a passage in which we are told that the saint himself and his companions built on the Kerry coast 'a very light little boat with a spine and ribs of pine, as the fashion is in those parts', but when they wanted a timber-built vessel they had to go to professional shipwrights to build it. This passage must be taken with caution however, as

Viking ship in full sail; reconstructed drawing by Liam de Paor

A Viking ship

it was written many centuries after the time of St Brendan, indeed some centuries after the Vikings had arrived with their special skill in the design and building of ships, and settled in the towns they founded at Dublin, Waterford, Wexford, Cork and Limerick. These had great influence on the economy of Ireland in the last century or so before the Norman invasion. They were merchants engaged in long distance trade along the coasts of Atlantic Europe, and they almost certainly stimulated new demands among the Irish and must have been quite potent agents of change in Irish society as a result. They were advanced in the design of long, broad, low-cut, clinker-built wooden sailing and rowing ships which were seaworthy and were yet adapted to coastal, estuary and river work. They opened up the Irish water-ways to these vessels in the ninth century and the tenth; by the twelfth century the Irish kings had learned from them how to use fleets for trans-porting armies on the Shannon and other major rivers and for concentrating their forces against an enemy's weak spot by use of ships and waterways. The Norse towns themselves each had their own fleet, and the twelfth century is full of reports of the comings and goings of these fleets along the Irish coasts. The Waterford and Dublin ships also appear to have established what amounted to a regular passenger service to Britain and the Continent by the time of the Norman invasion, so that more and more travellers were coming and going across the narrow seas.

In the matters of travel, transport and communications generally, as in almost any aspect of life we examine in the twelfth century, it would appear that Ireland on the eve of the Norman invasion had entered a period of rapid development and change. The Irish had made themselves known to Europe as travellers—pilgrims, missionaries, vagrants, wandering scholars—but as would appear from their writings they retained a fairly firm conviction, in their conservative way, that most matters were better ordered in Ireland. In travel as in most other things, we can find little indication of a desire to change until the eleventh century. After that the changes come rapidly; what is more to the point, the desire for change is evident: the beginning of a desire especially by new-style kings for roads, bridges, ships and merchants: a new kind of system of communications. This new system was emerging when the Normans came.

3 Transport and Communication in Medieval and Tudor Ireland

John G. Barry

A PASSAGE in the Norman French chanson *The Song of Dermot and the Earl,* a near contemporary source for the Norman Invasion of Ireland, tells us of the difficulty that Dermot McMurrough had in finding Henry II in France in 1166: he went 'up and down, forwards and back, he sent messages and made inquiries' until at last he caught up with him and gained audience.

This is one of the relatively few quotations relating to Irish history that is of revealing significance in the administrative history of medieval Europe. A society that seemed to be unaware of the whereabouts of the head of state at any given time seems almost incomprehensible to modern man; the author of *The Song* takes it quite for granted. In the sparsely populated Europe of the Middle Ages, the obstacles to communication were many. Apart from occasional proclamations there were no formal news media; for knowledge of distant events, everyone, whatever his rank, was obliged to rely on chance encounters. The roads and tracks were poor and unsafe. The only more or less regular service during the whole of the Middle Ages was that which linked Venice to Constantinople.

Paradoxically the roads were in constant use: where transport is difficult man goes to something more easily than he makes it come to him. In such conditions it was not possible to rule a kingdom from a capital city. The only way to control a territory was to ride through it incessantly in all directions. This was in fact precisely what Henry II was doing when Dermot McMurrough eventually found him somewhere in Aquitaine in southern France. Ireland was no exception. The king's justiciar and council of Anglo-

A farmer's waggon depicted in a medieval manuscript

Norman Ireland was endlessly itinerant. The council had no fixed centre. It is not until 1299 that we hear of a long seat of straw being bought for a council house, presumably in Dublin Castle. Throughout the whole of the Middle Ages, the council frequently met outside Dublin. Even parliament itinerated. As late as 1463 the parliament of the then shrunken colony which met at Waterford adjourned successively to Naas, Waterford and Dublin.

It was not only government that found it necessary to itinerate. Great lords both clerical and lay found it necessary to travel around from one estate to another. Medieval Ireland, like medieval Europe, was not wholly a money economy; much income was in kind. It was more convenient to consume the

A royal travelling coach from the same manuscript

produce on the spot, since to transport it to a common centre would be both inconvenient and expensive.

We have extant a comprehensive account of such a visitation of the see of Derry in 1397. Since the see was vacant it fell to Primate Coulton, the Archbishop of Armagh, to make the visitation. The Archbishop first arrived at the village of Cappagh and summoned before him the erenagh or chief of the sept farming church lands, in order to inform him that he was making the customary visitation. Since it seemed to the Archbishop that the village would not be able to support his retinue he decided to move on to the church at Ardstraw. He ordered the erenagh to provide beef for his retinue for the night in Ardstraw, and emphasised that this was in accordance with the custom by which they supplied the bishops of Derry in their visitation. The Archbishop continued on his journey while the erenagh followed after him to deliver a fat ox to his servants.

On arriving at Ardstraw the Archbishop called the vicar and erenaghs of the place before him and ordered them to make provision for his men and horses. He also demanded an effective guard for his entire retinue and their goods. Bread, butter, milk, meat and fuel for the men, together with corn and straw for the horses, were brought to every house where his men and horses were billeted. Guards were stationed around the village, especially around the house where the Archbishop was staying. All this was done at the expense of the erenaghs and residents of Ardstraw. On the following day he proceeded to Urney within the same diocese. On leaving Ardstraw he was provided, at the expense of the erenaghs and their septs, with seven horses which carried some of the paraphernalia of his retinue. The horses were returned when he reached Urney. This procedure, all clearly according to custom, was repeated with minor variations throughout the visitation. On Saturday 13 October 1397 the visitation proper was held in the choir of the cathedral at Derry. The Dean, Archdeacon, the Chapter, all the clergy and erenaghs were cited to appear before the Archbishop and show their letters of dignities, benefices, offices and orders, as well as deeds of lands and offices.

Ecclesiastical visitations of this kind were paralleled on the civil side by the custom known in Ireland as 'coshering' where the lay lord quartered his following on his dependents. This account of Archbishop Coulton's visitation makes it very clear that itineraries of this kind served the dual function of

A Gaelic ruler setting out on a journey on horseback

administration and of consumption of income in kind.

If local administrative and economic necessity were factors that kept the roads in constant use there were many others. The universal character of the church with Latin as a common language amongst educated priests and monks, together with the increasingly centralised administration both of the papacy and of the religious orders, which was a feature of the Middle Ages, ensured constant travelling not only within a local or national area, but throughout all of Christendom. The cleric eager for learning sometimes travelled all over Europe in search of education. This was particularly the case in Ireland since there was no university in the country throughout the Middle Ages. Both Irish and Anglo-Irish went abroad in considerable numbers to study. We find for instance that Thomas O'Colman, lector of the Franciscans at Armagh in 1375, had studied at Paris, Oxford and Cambridge.

Clerical affairs brought travellers into Ireland as well as inducing the Irish to travel abroad. Bishops in the purely Irish part of medieval Ireland had to deal with Irish rulers rather than with the King of England. In 1216 the great Pope Innocent III wrote to the King of Connacht, Cathal Crovderg O'Connor, requiring him to permit freedom of episcopal and abbatial elections. At the end of the same century Pope Boniface VIII sent the Bull *Clericis Laicos,* which forbade lay rulers to exact, or ecclesiastics to pay taxation without papal permission, to Nicholas Mac Maol Iosa, Archbishop of Armagh for publication. The Archbishop summoned O'Neill and the lords of Tir Eoghan before him and had the Bull read to them. They formally accepted it. It is a significant manifestation of the universal nature of Latin Christendom to find a Bull designed to prevent the exaction of extraordinary taxation of ecclesiastics by the rising national monarchies of western Europe being sent to the Archbishop of Armagh for use against the exactions of princes in one of the most conservative and remote societies of Christendom.

The centralised nature of Latin monasticism in the high Middle Ages, in particular that of the Cistercians, also contributed its quota of travellers to and from Ireland. There were many Cistercian houses in Ireland; they had been introduced before the Invasion, and it was incumbent on the abbots to attend the general chapter of the order which met annually at Citeaux. In turn each Cistercian abbey was obliged to receive a visitor, generally from its mother abbey. In 1217 the Abbot of Mellifont was deposed because, amongst other offences, he had refused to meet the visitors sent by the Abbot of Clairvaux to whom the reformation of the daughter house of Mellifont had been entrusted. There was to be further trouble in the order. In 1227 at a visitation carried out by two French abbots, the Cellarer of Mellifont and the Abbot of Baltinglass were deposed. In the next year Stephen de Lexington, Abbot of Stanley in England, to whom the task of reforming the order in Ireland had been entrusted by the Abbot of Clairvaux, carried out a general visitation of the Irish houses. The troubles of the Cistercians in Ireland, primarily caused by racial conflict, do not really concern us except in so far as they demonstrate the necessity for constant travel during the Middle Ages. An examination of other religious orders—the Friars Mendicant or the military religious order of the Knights Hospitallers—reveal a similar constant contact between Ireland, England and the Continent. Anglo-Irish knights of the Hospital, the Irish priory which was part of the English Langue of the Order, participated in the epic siege of Rhodes in 1480.

A particular feature of Gaelic Ireland was the manner in which the literary men of Gaelic Ireland passed readily both from the house of one chieftain to another and from monastery to monastery. Their itinerary extended as far as Gaelic Scotland which in literary matters was entirely under Irish domination through the whole medieval period. Some texts found in manuscripts were apparently written by Scottish scribes in Ireland, and the books of Scottish teachers, for example, contain tractates translated by Irish physicians. Some of them went even further afield. The Four Masters under the year 1213 tell us of the vicissitudes of Muireadhach O'Daly, a member of the great poetic family of Westmeath which had gradually scattered through the country in the Middle Ages. In this year Finn O'Brollaghan, O'Donnell's tax gatherer, behaved in what O'Daly considered to be an unmannerly way, in the course of his duties, in the poet's house at Lissadell in Sligo. O'Daly seized an axe and killed the tax gatherer at one blow. He then fled from O'Donnell's wrath to McWilliam Burke in Galway, from where he addressed a poem to O'Donnell in which he expresses some surprise at the way in which the chieftain was taking such a trivial incident.

> What reason for such wrath can be?
> The rascal bandied words with me
> I took an axe and hewed him down—
> Small matter for a prince's frown.

Italian bankers

38

O'Donnell did not accept this cavalier attitude to the matter and Muireadhach had to take refuge in Scotland. During his stay in Scotland he appears to have gone with the Scottish contingent on the Fifth Crusade which attacked Egypt, for poems of his exist written on board ship in the Adriatic on the way to the east. It is pleasing to learn that a series of poems eventually mollified the wrath of his lord, and he returned to Ireland. Another O'Daly poet of a rather different kind, Tadhg Crookshanks, a Franciscan, went abroad to study in the late fourteenth century. In his poem of farewell we see a very constant and long-standing motif of Irish religious feeling, the 'white martyrdom' of pilgrimage: 'For Christ's sake—though I make no boast thereof—have I left the people of the Gael whom I longed to have ever at my hand, and for love of him have I deserted Eire.'

Trade was perhaps the greatest single factor in travel. In the early Middle Ages, in the absence of representatives to whom he could delegate the task of buying and selling, every merchant was perforce a traveller. There is evidence of trade in pre-Norman Ireland, but in Gaelic Ireland itself no true towns existed. The centres of commercial importance were the Norse settlements of Dublin, Wexford, Waterford, Cork and Limerick. The Normans in fact arrived in Ireland on the crest of a wave of municipal development in western Europe that was primarily due to a growth in commerce following the first crusade. The Normans were great traders; they took over the Norse towns and established a number of new urban settlements which were in course of time to become true towns.

A flourishing export trade developed in Ireland in the thirteenth century. Ireland was a major source of supply for the king's Scottish wars towards the end of the century. Indeed a recent interpretation of the Edward Bruce episode in the early fourteenth century is that Bruce's devastation of Ireland, which the Irish annalists denounce so bitterly, is to be explained by regarding his invasion more as a foray to destroy an important source of supply for the English king, rather than as a serious attempt to establish an independent kingdom of Ireland.

As well as trade with England there was a flourishing Irish trade with the continent of Europe. By the middle of the thirteenth century there were regular commercial relations between Ireland and France, Flanders and the Italian towns. The Italians were by far the dominant element of the continental people doing business in Ireland. The Italian merchants came chiefly from

Spanish wine ships

Lucca, Florence and Lombardy. In 1280 we find Perceval of Lucca trading in wool and hides in Ireland, and in 1285 the custody of the Irish wool trade is given to the firm of Ricarde from the same town. The rapidly expanding wool trade in Italy and Flanders at this time made the raising of sheep and the export of wool a lucrative business.

A flourishing import as well as export trade developed in prosperous thirteenth-century Anglo-Norman Ireland. From the very earliest times wine had been imported into Ireland. It was of course indispensable for the celebration of Mass. When the Normans settled in Ireland, however, the use of wine became much more general, and the trade in consequence received a decided impetus. In the thirteenth century most of the wine came from Gascony and was shipped from Rouen, Bordeaux or La Rochelle to Ireland. In 1281 we find a Gascon merchant selling wine in Dublin, and in 1288 Geoffrey Brun paid £20 for ten hogsheads of wine in Galway for dispatch to the royal castles in Connacht. French wine continued to be used throughout the Middle Ages, but by the fifteenth century a very substantial trade in Spanish wine had also developed.

As well as wine a very substantial import trade developed in other commodities which could not be produced at home. These included spices, always popular in the Middle Ages because they concealed the taste of meat and fish that must often have been high: condiments like salt and pepper, fruit, such as almonds, figs and raisins; coal, lead, tin, axes, nails, spades, and certain finer types of cloth. In the sixteenth century we find the ladies of Galway wearing French hoods. Their fashions impressed the Lord Deputy, Sir John Perrott, as decidedly extravagant. The gentlemen of Galway were not far behind the ladies in their desire to be fashionably dressed. They appear to have employed English tailors regularly. It was only in the tailoring business that outside craftsmen were admitted to practise their trade in Galway. Apparently in the sixteenth as in the twentieth century the dictates of France inspired women's fashions in headgear, and English tailoring had acquired something of the reputation that it enjoys today.

Inland, towns developed around castles, whether founded by royal charter as was Athlone, or by such lords as the Marshalls at Kilkenny or Kildare. All the inland towns which were to become of any real commercial importance were situated on navigable waterways. These were of paramount importance in the transport conditions of the age. By contrast with today, travel was much faster by sea or navigable river than by land. Sixty to ninety miles a day was not an exceptional record for a ship provided that the winds were not too unfavourable. On land the normal distance covered by a caravan of merchants or by a nobleman moving from castle to castle amounted to between twenty and twenty-five miles. Goods could also be carried in greater bulk and consequently more economically on a ship than on a pack horse or mule. In 1173 when the Normans under Raymond Le Gros defeated the forces of Dermot McCarthy, King of South Munster, and plundered Lismore, they sent the cattle captured in the foray along the coast road to Waterford, but they loaded the rest of the booty on to thirteen ships which they sent down the Blackwater to reach Waterford by sea.

It was naturally in the interest of towns to improve communications since they were primarily trading centres. We find them from time to time being given the right to raise tolls on commodities not only to wall themselves,

41

Ships carrying provisions into Waterford for Richard II's army in Ireland

but to build bridges. Most of these bridges would have been made of wood. We have pictures drawn by Richarus Barthelett about 1600 of wooden bridges, including those of the north and south gate bridges across the Ulster Blackwater which gave access to the Charlemont fort. From such references in the Annals as 'the plank bridge' at Killaloe it is clear that wooden bridges were being built in Ireland as early as the eleventh century. The Annals of Ulster under the year 1190 refer to 'a very good bridge of wood that was made by O'Brien across the Shannon'. Professor M. J. O'Kelly has examined and reported in detail on the structure of one such bridge over the Cashen river in Kerry. It is a work of quite sophisticated construction.

Although the native Irish were not completely excluded from the towns, nevertheless they were almost exclusively English enclaves. We have all heard of the corporation statute of Galway that 'neither O nor Mac shall strut or swagger through the streets of Galway'. In the later Middle Ages, however, the citizens of the towns were dependent in many cases on the native Irish both for the bulk of their exports and for the very necessities of life. The wool, hides, tallow, and provisions that made up the bulk of the exports from Irish towns had to be bought largely from them, and the Irish bought from the townsmen. Galway paid O'Brien, Lord of the Aran Islands, an annual tribute of wine for protection to shipping in the bay of Galway. O'Toole in Leinster wrote to Richard II in 1395, 'without buying and selling I can in no way live ... I would that you would send me your letters patent, so that for the future I may enjoy free buying and selling in your fairs and towns'.

All this trade involved constant traffic on the roads and waterways. From market to market the country was traversed by roads and waterways. Where the English armies had not previously penetrated in the sixteenth century the Deputy was surprised to see the highways and paths so well beaten. Another sixteenth-century account refers to an open road that ran between Rathcoull, probably Rathconnell near Mullingar in Westmeath, and Queylan, used only by the 'Irish enemies of the King', where trains of bullocks and horse tracks of merchandise and victuals were to be seen, to the profit of these 'Irish enemies'. The local corporation statutes of towns such as Galway, regulating trade, forbidding for instance the sale of crossbows, guns and powder to the native Irish, were constantly broken, and broken often by the very men who made them.

Beyond the roads lay bogs, thickets, forests, and the rough and treacherous ground of a country undrained and by modern standards, overgrown. Progress along these roads was difficult enough; outside of them, particularly for large bodies of people such as troops on the move, it was almost impossible. It is not surprising therefore that the pass is an ever recurring theme in medieval and Tudor Irish military history.

A pass was not just a narrow way between hills or mountains; the term was also applied to roads through forests, or causeways often wooden, through

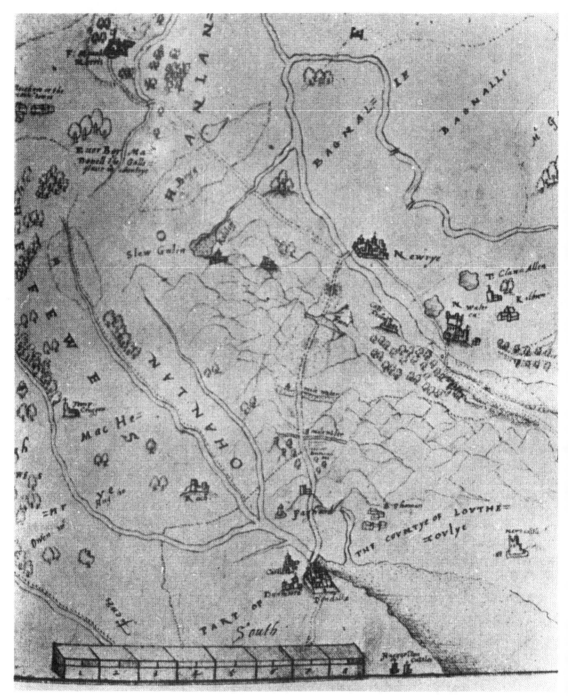

Early map showing the terrain of Moyra Pass

bogs. As early as 1169 the progress of the Normans was delayed by MacGilla-patrick who cut trenches across the forest paths and put up ramparts behind them. He erected stockades of wattle on top of the ramparts, and fought the Normans from behind these formidable defences. In the same year Dermot McMurrough prepared the same kind of defences when the High King advanced against him at his fortress near Ferns. This district, still known as the Dubbry or Dubh-tir, black or dark country, was then covered with woods; hence the name. In order to keep attackers to the paths, and to prevent infiltration into the woods which might outflank his forces, Dermot plashed the margins of the pathways; that is he made impenetrable hedgerows of the undergrowth on either side by interweaving cut branches between the growing shrubs and saplings.

Four hundred years later there are many references in sixteenth-century documents to show that in Munster, in Ulster, in the Midlands, wherever there were battles, the Irish still used these tactics. Trenches, stockades and plashed woods were still commonplace because from the twelfth to the sixteenth century the Irish terrain did not change to any great extent. There were in the end as there had been in the beginning, deep woods, much rough ground, many mountains and roads; tracks or paths which were by modern standards few, narrow and difficult. Progress away from these roads was an uncertain matter, not ordinarily attempted by travellers. It could seldom have been attempted by armies. The result was the abiding danger of the pass.

Some of the hardest fighting of the nine years' war that was finally to subjugate Gaelic Ireland, at the end of the sixteenth century, took place at passes of one kind or another. O'Neill's victory at Clontibret took place where the road ran through a bog. The most severe and prolonged fighting of the war was at Moyra Pass or Bealach an Mhaighre, the celebrated Gap of the North, the defile in the hills below Slieve Gullion in Co. Armagh, through which the railway now runs from Dublin to Belfast. The road through the pass in the sixteenth century, according to an Elizabethan commentator, was 'a broken cawsey', i.e. causeway beset on both sides by bogs, where 'the Irish might skip but where the English could not go'. It was naturally one of the most difficult passes in Ireland. When Mountjoy attempted to force this in 1600, his secretary Fynes Morrison said that from mountain to mountain, from wood to wood, and from bog to bog the Irish had raised long traverses with huge and high flankers of great stones staked on both sides

45

with wattled palisades. Where there were trees on either side of the track the Irish had plashed the undergrowth and the trees, in the same way that McMurrough and MacGillapatrick had done more than four hundred years earlier. 'It would not have been easy,' said Captain Nicholas Dawtrey, an English officer who served there, 'for swine to pass through, much less men'.

If the state of the roads produced in some ways the same kind of military situation at the end of the Middle Ages as at the beginning, neither did any other kind of transport change to any great extent. Transport was not appreciably quicker at the end of the Middle Ages than it was at the beginning. In 1558, in times of peace, Sussex, the Lord Deputy, took two days to travel the sixty odd miles from Limerick to Galway.

The obstacles and dangers of the road in the Middle Ages in Ireland, as in the rest of Europe, in no way prevented travel, but it made each journey, whether that of pilgrim or merchant, civil or ecclesiastical courier, an expedition, almost an adventure. Men under pressure of need did not fear to undertake long journeys, but they did not travel for pleasure and shrank from those comings and goings within a narrow radius which in other civilisations form the texture of daily life. Humbler people in settled occupations rarely left their parish or town. On the other hand scarcely any remote little place did not have some intermittent contact through the sort of continuous movement that affected the whole of society. In the words of the distinguished authority Marc Bloch: 'If, according to the angle from which it is viewed, the civilisation of feudal Europe appears sometimes remarkably universalist, sometimes particularist in the extreme, the principal source of this contradiction lay in the conditions of communication, conditions which favoured the distant propagation of very general currents of influence as much as they discouraged, in any particular place, the standardising effects of neighbourly intercourse'.

4 The Age of the Stage Coach

J. L. McCracken

A LOT of attention was paid to road building in eighteenth-century Ireland. The country was at peace, trade was expanding; the need for easier means of communications was being felt. By the last quarter of the century Ireland was well provided with good roads. Between then and the building of the railways, horsedrawn transport enjoyed a golden age and the stage coaches held pride of place on the roads.

Many people of course still moved about on foot or on horseback. Any sort of transport was beyond the means of many and there were also those who walked from choice or when necessity arose. Such a one was the young Frenchman De Latocnaye who walked round Ireland in 1796–97 armed with an umbrella and carrying his possessions in a handkerchief slung on the end of a sword stick. And John O'Donovan of the first ordnance survey walked the twenty-two Irish miles from Omagh to Enniskillen when the coach left early without him. He arrived, he says, 'without feeling in the least fatigued, vexation having animated me all along.' As for riding, it had great advantages. It was faster, cheaper and less troublesome, especially in the more remote parts of the country where post horses might be hard to get and where the roads could be bad. Quite a number of the travellers who visited and wrote about Ireland at this time went on horseback. So too did the locals: the members of the Irish Bar, for example, and the linen merchants in the north who were apparently so wedded to the saddle that they even appeared at balls in boots and spurs 'to the great annoyance of the ladies'.

Gentlemen also travelled on horseback but they had their own carriages as well. Strangers noted the variety of well turned-out private vehicles in and

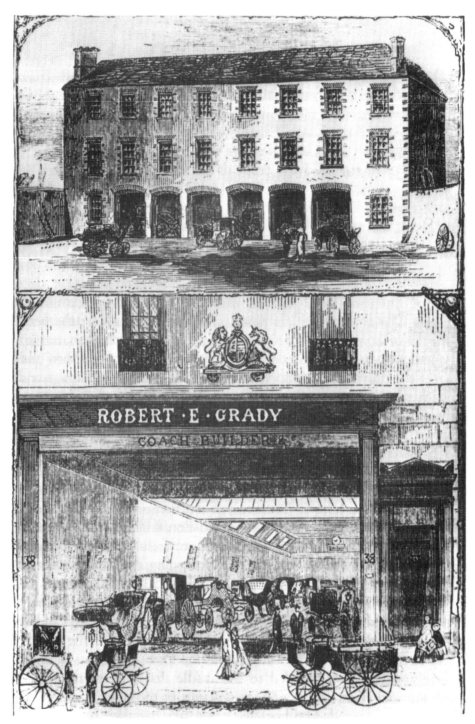

A Dublin coachworks in the late eighteenth century

48

NELSON PLACE CARRIAGE WORKS,
CORK.

ESTABLISHED 1810.

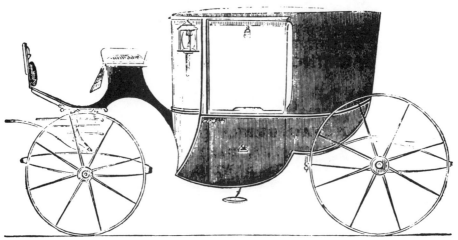

THE MODEL BROUGHAM, AS EXHIBITED AT THE
DUBLIN INTERNATIONAL EXHIBITION, 1865.
CLASS B, SECTION 5 C.

JAMES JOHNSON

Solicits inspection of his extensive and elegant assortment of New Carriages, which are made by First-class Workmen, most of whom have had experience in the First London Houses in the Trade; and using none but best materials, he is enabled to produce Carriages of the lightest possible construction, of the newest and most approved Designs, equal to the best London Build, and at prices which defy competition.

N.B.—Carriages Jobbed, with or without the option of Purchase.

Detailed Estimates and Designs forwarded to any part of the Kingdom on application, and the strictest Economy and Punctuality observed in all Repairs.

The full value allowed for old Carriages taken in Exchange, or Sold on Commission.

49

An inside jaunting car

about the towns. Coaches were imported from Britain: £787 worth of them in 1736 and £3,930 worth in 1783. There was also a coachbuilding industry in Ireland which grew with the development of public transport. John Hutton established a firm in 1779 that lasted into the twentieth century. Coachbuilding was giving employment to between 1,700 and 2,000 men in Dublin in 1799 and this did not include car, gig and chaise makers. By 1849 there were twenty-five carriage works in Dublin alone.

The hire of a post chaise was another course open to those who could afford it, but even on much-frequented routes Irish post chaises were dilapidated. A traveller who came off the packet at Donaghadee could find himself journeying to Belfast in a vehicle which was neither wind-proof nor water-proof, with luggage piled on the roof and made secure with hayrope and old cord 'which traverse the windows in several directions to where it is fastened and in some cases helps to hold the doors shut.' Off the main roads chaises and post horses were not easy to come by and as Sir Richard Colt Hoare said, a traveller's purse could be taxed and his time lost. An account of posting and turnpike charges in 1826 shows how expensive a mode of travelling this was. The cost of horses and boys at each stage was usually about £2 and this meant that the journey from Kilkenny to Cork via Fermoy, for example, cost £8 10s. 6d. with a further 14s. for turnpike tolls.

It was a lot cheaper to hire a jaunting car which is what the ordinary traveller had to do if he wanted to get off the beaten track. The jaunting car was peculiar to Ireland; it was cheap—as little as 6d. a mile in places—and it was fairly widespread. But it was not the most comfortable of vehicles; the violent motion when the horse galloped amused some people but made others feel sick.

Dublin had always a greater variety of vehicles for hire. An early one was the Ringsend car, a one-horse affair with the seat suspended on a leather strap between the shafts. Another was the noddy, a low covered vehicle with the shafts well up, which nodded as it moved. The driver sat, we are told, 'so that the rump of the horse is at his mouth, and his rump at the mouth of the person in the chaise'; an arrangement described as 'indelicate'. However we

A more elegant jaunting car

A noddy

are assured that only 'the lowest orders of citizens' used the noddy; there was a proverb 'Elegance and ease, like a shoeblack in a noddy.' Then there was the jingle which was described as resembling as much of a coach as remained after the doors, the upper sides and the roof had been removed. It was mounted very high on four large slender wheels and drawn by a single horse. As it moved it made a jingling noise. The principal stand for these cars was at the end of Baggot Street and they plied mainly to the Pigeon House and Blackrock at the rate of 6d. a person, provided they had a full complement of six passengers. Though they were not much to look at they were very popular and 'persons of the first respectability' frequently rode in them. There were hackney coaches too, similar to the ones in London, though less comfortable and clean, and jaunting cars which eventually replaced the other vehicles. One other mode of transport in Dublin was the sedan chair. At one time every family of any consequence had two or three of these and public chairs were very numerous: in 1771 when the total number of carriages of all kinds licensed to ply in Dublin was 300 the number of licensed chairs was 400. Sedans were still plying in Dublin in the 1830s and Cork, Belfast and Waterford also had their chairs.

For those who had occasion to travel in the country, the coming of the stage coaches effected a major change. As early as 1718 a twice-weekly coach service between Dublin and Kinnegad was announced. By 1737 coaches were running twice a week from Dublin to Drogheda, Kilkenny and Kinnegad and once a week to Athlone. Three years later the first stage coach to Belfast went into service and a second one drawn by 'six able horses' joined it in the following year. But one of them disappeared almost at once and the other did not survive for long. Another attempt at establishing a link with Belfast was made in 1752 but the service north of Newry was withdrawn a couple of years later and it was not until 1788 that Belfast became permanently linked to the capital. By that time coaches were leaving Dublin two or three days a week for twelve different destinations. In 1784 a separate Post Office was established for Ireland and in 1789 mail coach services on the English pattern came into operation, in addition to the stage coach services. The Southern Mail Coach left Dublin for Cork at 10 o'clock every night and the Northern

A sedan chair

View into D'Olier Street and Westmoreland Street from Carlisle Bridge

Mail Coach for Belfast and Donaghadee at 10.30 p.m. At the beginning of the new century there were mail coach services to Longford, Limerick and Athlone as well. By 1805 Derry, Enniskillen, Sligo, Cavan, Dungannon and Waterford had been added to the places served, and by 1834, when the railway age was just beginning, there were twenty-eight mail coach lines in the country and forty coaches were operating out of Dublin.

There had been a time when it was usual for anyone intending to travel from Cork or Galway to Dublin to settle his affairs, make his will and take leave of his friends before setting out. With the coming of the coaches, travel lost much of its terror and isolation was ended. A writer in the *Irish Farmer's and Gardiner's Magazine* in November 1834 recalled the time, some five years before, when the only public conveyance passing through Omagh had been the Dublin-Derry mail. Now the traveller had the choice of two coaches and two caravans daily to Derry, two coaches, besides the mail, to Dublin and no less than three conveyances to Enniskillen, though only a year or two before no one had thought of running even a car there.

The excellent condition of most of the Irish roads made for ease of movement. Only the turnpike roads—and there were not many of them—came in for serious criticism. English visitors were astonished to find anything in Ireland better than in England but they were in no doubt about the roads: one of them said the Irish roads were surpassed only by those of Sweden and another that the famous Macadam roads of England were not a whit better. The Irish roads were well made and there were few trees and hedges to keep the wind and sun from drying them after rain. In some counties they were well sign-posted: Meath, Louth and Fermanagh are mentioned. One traveller praised Lord Blayney for putting up sign-posts at the cross roads round Castleblayney 'not so high as to be visible to hawks and eagles only.' In other parts there were no sign-posts because, it was said, the poor would have cut them down for fuel as soon as they had been put up. But what really distinguished the Irish from the English roads and saved them from being cut to pieces was the absence of heavy goods traffic. The common cart was a primitive vehicle drawn by one horse, mounted low on solid wooden wheels about two or two and a half feet in diameter fixed to an iron or wooden axle-tree which turned with the wheels. The cart was drawn so close to the horse that it became extremely filthy. The whole thing weighed not much over a couple of hundredweight and carried, as one writer contemputously said, about the load of three English wheel barrows. There was also a superior type of cart—sometimes called a Scotch car or cart because it was borrowed from Scotland—higher from the ground, with low sides, also drawn by one horse, which was used for carrying goods longer distances. Though we hear of droves of these carts on the roads neither was capable of doing the damage to road surfaces that the great English waggons weighing up to three tons did.

Travellers by the Irish coaches, then, were spared the inconveniences that arose from bad roads but they were not immune from hazards and discomforts. In the early days of coaching highwaymen constituted a real danger. At the beginning of the nineteenth century the mail coaches started to carry two armed guards. The first mail coaches had only one. One of the inducements held out to travellers on the Dublin-Cork run in 1808 was that a newly-acquired coach was copper-lined and therefore bullet proof. Thomas McTear of Belfast tells us that on his first trip to Dublin sometime before 1820 the mail coach, in addition to its two guards armed with polished brass blunder-busses and loaded pistols, had an escort of six armed dragoons from Newry to

Dundalk and from Dundalk to Drogheda to deal with the highwaymen who frequented the mountain road from Newry and the district of Lurgan Green, south of Dundalk. These precautions were not unwarranted. The Drogheda coach was robbed at Santry on a September afternoon in 1773 by two young men who took money and watches from all the passengers except a priest. Thirteen armed men plundered the Limerick mail near Maryborough in 1799 and four of them rode off on the coach horses. In 1807 the *Cock of the North* coach was held up near Newry by ten men who robbed the thirteen passengers and stole the driver's whip to prevent pursuit. In the summer of the next year Edward Brennan was infesting the mountains of Tipperary and the eastern parts of Cork. The Enniskillen mail was robbed at Dunshaughlin by fourteen armed men in 1815 but when it was attacked again at the same place a year later the two guards succeeded in clearing a road block and saving the mails.

By the second decade of the nineteenth century highway robbery had been stamped out and thereafter road users in Ireland suffered no molestation, however disturbed the country might be politically. 'There is not any country under heaven,' said a visitor in the eighteen forties, 'in which a stranger may travel with more perfect safety.' The only complaint thereafter was about the swarms of beggars who surrounded the coaches on arrival and departure. But as one traveller pointed out, however earnest their entreaties, they were never rude. No man ever had to complain of being insulted by them.

There were still dangers to be faced even when travelling by mail coach. The mail coaches were the aristocrats of the road and could claim right of way. As in England, they were run by contractors who provided the vehicles and coachmen and operated the services. The guards were employees of the Post Office and were paid from £150 to £200 a year. For many years the mail contract was held by the Dublin firm of Bourne and Hartley. They were succeeded by their associate Purcell from 1838 to 1842 and then the contract was lost to Scotland. Irish coachmen had the reputation of being more civil and attentive than their English counterparts but the service was not so efficient as in England. The coaches were less regularly inspected with the result that things were always going wrong, the distances between the stages were greater and a less uniform pace was maintained. Sometimes, we are told, they would 'linger twenty minutes or half an hour at the door of some whiskey house, and afterwards make up the time lost by the most impetuous and dangerous driving'. Coachmen and guards were better friends than in England and the result was that 'as long as there are two glasses of whiskey on the road, the English traveller will never hear (what he so often hears in his own country) the voice of the guard in the execution of his duty.' What this sort of thing could lead to is shown by the experience of a traveller in 1812. He joined the Newry coach, *The Old Cock,* at Balbriggan. It was heavily laden with ten passengers inside and more outside; the front wheel was shattered, the body work was in bad repair, but the coachman was determined to keep the lead over the *Cock of the North* which was coming along behind with an equally heavy load. As they went down a steep hill after leaving Dundalk the wheel broke, and the passengers had no alternative but to extricate themselves from the ditch and walk the rest of the way to Newry. On another occasion the same traveller experienced bad time-keeping. When he booked a seat on the Drogheda coach in Dublin he was told to be there at 7 a.m. precisely because the coach would not wait a moment longer even for King George himself. In fact it waited an hour for a little hunch-backed passenger.

But there were discomforts attendant on coach travel for which the

The hazards of stage-coach travel

operators were not entirely to blame. The experiences of two travellers, one an outside and the other an inside passenger, will illustrate the point. John O'Donovan on his way to Derry in October 1834 joined the coach at Maghera. As they passed through Glenshane, he said, 'wind-driven showers wet us to the skin and shattered our umbrellas.' He got to Derry just in time to join the *Fair Trader* for Enniskillen. It carried twenty-eight passengers, ten inside and eighteen outside, 'noisy and half-inebriated fellows.' The rain and wind continued and his umbrella 'only served to collect the passing shower and drop it upon my legs and thighs and into my shoes.' At Strabane he got down to look for a glass of whiskey 'to put the chilled stream of life into artificial circulation' but when he saw the rush for the few seats that had been vacated he scrambled back again. He was too late to regain his former seat and had to fix himself on the top of a trunk that towered over the upper seats. The final blow came between Strabane and Newtownstewart when a wheel slipped into the ditch and he was catapulted from his lofty perch.

The other traveller, John Gamble, on his way north in 1810, joined the Derry mail at Drogheda for Monaghan. The coach came in at one in the morning. When he got into it he found two women sitting side by side so he stretched himself on the opposite seat to sleep. But presently three large men appeared and he was squeezed in between two of them. It was a very warm night but they were muffled up in great coats and before long perspiration was running down Gamble's face. To add to his discomfort one of the women who complained of rheumatism kept chewing garlic and the men's breath reeked of punch. After a few miles the man on his left fell asleep and began to snore like a rhinoceros and his head kept bumping against Gamble. The man on the other side started to sing in a monotonous tone like the drone of a pair of bagpipes. After he had gone through *Listen to the Voice of Love* and several other songs including one with upwards of forty verses, Gamble angrily asked him how he thought anyone could sleep. 'And is it sleep you are talking about, my honey,' was the reply. 'Faith if it's that you want you should have stayed at home in your neat comfortable bed and laid yourself snug between your two sheets; the devil a soul here would have thought of wakening you.' Gamble thought it better not to pursue the argument—the man had the fist of an ox. However in a minute or two he changed to a whistle. Eventually Gamble, in a state of exhaustion, fell asleep leaving his companion in the middle of *Rule Britannia*.

Even when all went well, travelling by stage coach was slow and expensive. The first coaches from Dublin to Belfast in 1740 spent three days on the journey in winter and two in summer and in the early years of the nineteenth century the Cork mail took thirty-one hours and the Limerick coach twenty-one hours. It is true that there was an improvement as time went on but on the eve of the railway age the mail coach to Belfast still took eleven and a half hours, to Cork eighteen and a half hours and to Limerick fourteen hours. As for fares, it cost, for example, 8s. 8d. for an inside and 6s. 6d. for an outside seat from Dublin to Drogheda in 1810; 8s. 6d. for an outside seat from Belfast to Newry in 1828; and 27s. 6d. for an inside and 15s. for an outside seat from Dublin to Belfast in 1838. In addition the coachman, but not the guard on a mail coach, expected a tip.

The traveller by road in the coaching age had two useful reference books at his disposal. In the autumn of 1776 two cartographers, George Taylor and Andrew Skinner, who had already done the highways of Scotland and the post road from London to Bath, submitted a plan for mapping the roads of Ireland and invited subscriptions from the gentlemen of the country. The outcome was a book of 288 pages tracing the route between places in the manner of the maps provided by modern motoring organisations. The first route for example covers the road from Dublin to Donaghadee in six pages, two of them double-columned. The maps, in addition to showing towns and villages and the distances between them, marked gentlemen's houses, churches, inns, spas, barracks, race-courses and a few antiquities. The *Roads of Ireland,* first published in 1778, was reissued in a revised edition in 1783. This was followed by a topographical description without maps compiled with the help of subscribers to the map volume, who had been invited to send particulars of their estates and of any curiosities in their neighbourhood. The new book, called the *Post chaise companion,* was published in 1784 and reissued several times. Route by route it provided an account of the things of interest the traveller could see. The maps themselves were not reissued again but they continued to be used well into the 1800s though by that time they were becoming outdated because of the rapid advances in road construction.

Increasing traffic on the roads led to big improvements in posting establishments and inns. Dr Twiss who made a tour of Ireland in 1775 complained about the lack of stages for horses but by 1806 another traveller found only two out of fifty-seven inns he visited to be without post-horses. The inns

The

POST-CHAISE COMPANION:

OR,

Travellers Directory;

through

IRELAND.

Containing a new and Accurate Description
of the direct and principal Cross-Roads, with
particulars of the Noblemen and Gentlemen's
Seats, Cities, Towns, Parks, Natural Curiosities,
Antiquities, Castles, Ruins, Manufactures,
Loughs, Glens, Harbours, &c. &c.

———— Forming ————

An Historical & descriptive Account of the Kingdom.

To which is added,

a *DICTIONARY*, or

Alphabetical Tables.

Shewing the distance of all the Principal
Cities, Boroughs, Market and Sea port Towns,
in Ireland from each other.

Darling Scrip.   **Dublin**   J. Duff Sculp.

Printed for the Author, N.º 6, Dame Street.
1786.

themselves had once had a bad reputation. The country was poor, travellers were few and the gentry were so hospitable that 'respectable persons may travel from one end of Ireland to the other without putting their foot within the threshold of an inn.' We find complaints of dirty beds, cupboards and drawers without handles and slovenly servants. 'Wretched and miserable hog-styes' and 'filthy and disgusting' are the sort of terms applied to them. But by the coaching era things had improved: new inns had been built and good ones were to be found even in out-of-the-way places. Thackeray found 'the prettiest, comfortablest inn in Ireland' in Westport and there was a well-conducted one at Ballygawley, Co. Tyrone. A visitor in 1810 had an excellent dinner of boiled goose with onion sauce. The outside was shabby but it was decently furnished, clean, with geraniums in the windows and prints on the walls, including one of Sophia, fallen from horseback, taken from *Tom Jones*. 'There was', we are told, 'a capital display of limbs in this print. It was harmless, however, the legs were as thick as a citizen's in a dropsy and the face as frightful as Medusa's.' When the guest asked the landlord for a book he sent up Baxter's *Call to the unconverted* and Willison's *On the sacrament*. Another soberly-conducted establishment was Jones' Hotel in Derry. It could produce a good dinner and a tolerable pint of port but it had bibles in every room, dark gloomy passages, a severe figure of a landlord in seedy black and was 'almost as gay as a family vault'. To a man who had sat on an outside seat of a stage coach all night, breakfast was an important meal and Irish inn breakfasts were well spoken of. Toast was never served as in England, swimming in greasy butter; it was cut into thin slices and put on the table with fresh butter. Tea or coffee, two eggs, bread of every variety and as much cold meat as you wanted was the stock fare, but if you preferred a steak to the cold meat you could have one. The coming of the railways put paid to many a coaching inn. For example, Slane, the second posting stage north from Dublin on the Derry route, had a 'large and commodious' hotel but by 1858 it had been turned into a private house and there was no hotel in the village.

Who used the coaches? The impression at the time was that a great many people did. Irish coaches seem always to have been full to overflowing. The first mail coaches had taken only five passengers, four inside and one outside, but as the coaches got larger they came to carry well over twenty people, and this enabled them to deal with considerable numbers. In 1834, the year in which Ireland's first railway was opened, the mail coaches from Dublin

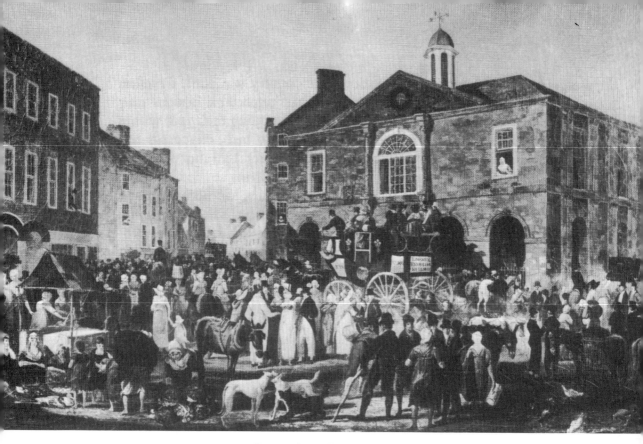

The North Cork–Limerick stage coach in 1820

carried over 4,000 people to Belfast, over 3,000 on each of the two routes to Cork and over 3,000 to Derry, Enniskillen, Galway, Sligo, Limerick and Waterford. These figures of course give only a partial picture of the volume of traffic; in addition there were the travellers by stage coach and by the public cars which were so important that they will be dealt with in another chapter.

As to what sort of people the coach users were, we get occasional glimpses of them in the writings of contemporaries: a man going to look at a mare and another going to examine a setter dog; a green-coated policeman with his carbine; three sailors on the roof of the *Skibbereen Industry;* a priest educated at Salamanca; a man from New York; an English actress. John Wilkinson went from Athlone to Dublin by stage coach in November 1775 in the company of an elderly lady of some fashion and her maid, the son of a nobleman, a buxom young lady from Roscommon and a country squire

62

from Galway who devoted his attentions to the young lady and sang to her in Irish. When Thackeray travelled by coach from Ballinasloe to Dublin he had as his companions a clergyman, a guard, a Scottish farmer, a butcher, a bookseller's hack, a lad bound for Maynooth and another for Trinity. At Moate where the butcher and the farmer got out four more Maynooth students joined the coach. 'A varied, pleasant party enough', was his comment.

By the early 1830s the writing was on the wall for the stage coaches. In January 1834 a steam carriage made a brief appearance on the streets of Dublin. In December of the same year the railway from Dublin to Dún Laoghaire—Kingstown as it was then—was opened to the public. The following April the mail was carried by train for the first time. Passenger traffic by mail coach from Dublin to Kingstown fell from 5,800 in 1834 to 1,200 in 1835. The coaching age did not come to an abrupt end. The spread of the railways was a slow process and the coaches continued to feed the railheads and to bridge the gaps. As late as 1855 when the bulk of the mail was leaving Dublin by train—though it might have to finish its journey by road— there were still mail coaches running out of Dublin. Nevertheless by that time the age of the stage coach was clearly at an end.

5 The Transport Revolution: Canals and River Navigations

W. A. McCutcheon

U P UNTIL the middle of the eighteenth century the only means of travel and communication in Ireland had been by road; the slow movement of goods, spasmodic troop forays and a trickle of internal passenger traffic between towns, and from country seat to capital, were the main strands in a pattern of movement taking place on road surfaces which until 1750 left much to be desired. However, the development of inland navigation in Britain and the vital contribution which water transport made to the Industrial Revolution soon had its effect in Ireland and in a country well-endowed with natural water-courses and great inland seas it was but natural that canal construction should be taken up on a large scale as the century progressed. At the dawn of the canal age in Ireland around 1730, the facilities for internal social and commercial intercourse were severely hampered by the inadequacy of the road system and the avenues of movement afforded by the various canals constructed between 1730 and 1860 did much to shape the evolution of trade, industry and population within that period.

Though several proposals to build canals in Ireland were made between 1690 and 1725 these proved abortive and it was not until 1731 that work began on the Newry Canal linking one of Ireland's chief maritime ports with the inland basin around Lough Neagh by means of a cut connecting Carlingford Lough with the Upper Bann, near Portadown. This navigation was completed in 1742 and ranks as the first true summit-level canal in the British Isles, ante-dating by about twenty years both the Sankey Cut at St Helen's and the Bridgewater Canal at Manchester.

In the north the Newry Canal was soon followed by the Tyrone and Lagan

Navigations, begun in 1733 and 1756 respectively, and in the south work began in the 1750s on the Grand Canal, the Shannon Navigation and the Barrow and Boyne Navigations. Thus, within thirty years a major programme of canal construction was under way in Ireland, a programme made possible only through the unbridled generosity of the Irish Parliament which between 1730 and 1787 granted upwards of £800,000 from public funds for canal works in Ireland. To appreciate fully the reasons prompting this

The Grand Canal Company's hotel at Portobello harbour, c. 1805

staggering outlay it is necessary to examine the general state of public finances in Ireland at that time, for it is here rather than in the demands of economic circumstances that one finds the explanation.

By the last quarter of the eighteenth century, a period of feverish canal construction and speculation, Great Britain was already a great manufacturing region with major areas of important mineral deposits and heavy industry for which canals provided an ideal means of inter-communication. From ports such as Liverpool, Glasgow, Bristol, Hull and London, canals provided direct contacts with expanding industrial hinterlands and did much to mould the patterns of industrial location and population distribution. Ireland, on the other hand, remained predominantly agricultural in character, a country in which the only traffic in minerals was an internal distribution from points of import. There were few raw materials beyond the produce of the land, for which inland water transport was ideally suited, and the peasant population was quite unable to support regular passenger services.

However, in the eighteenth century the basis of Irish revenue law was certain legislation of Charles II which provided that in return for the Crown foregoing the full benefit of the lands forfeit after the rebellion of 1641, the king should be granted a legal, hereditary revenue. The most important sources of this were, first, the Crown Rents arising from the land confiscations of Henry VIII and from the counties forfeited after the Earl of Tyrone's rebellion in the reign of Elizabeth I; second, the Quit Rents arising out of property forfeited after the rebellion of 1641; third, the 'Hearth Money'; and, fourth, the excise and customs duties and licences for selling spirits, wine and ale.[1]

A number of attempts were made by the Irish Parliament to gain control of this hereditary revenue in the eighteenth century. All these attempts were unsuccessful but to redress the balance the Irish Parliament kept local public expenditure as high as possible so that the Crown always had to resort to the English Parliament for funds to maintain a semblance of governmental control over Ireland. It soon became the custom of the Irish Parliament to grant large sums each session, nominally for public works such as the encouragement of industry, bridge construction, and canal and river navigation works but in many cases for the private advancement of members of parliament and their friends. Henceforth there was an additional, personal inducement to embark on canal-building schemes, and the full development of the Irish canal system dates from this time.

To return to the era of canal construction, the first Newry Ship Canal was completed in 1769, the Lagan Navigation, from Belfast to Lough Neagh, in 1784, the Tyrone Navigation in 1787, the Strabane Canal in 1796, the main line of the Grand Canal in 1811 and the Royal Canal in 1817. Navigation works on the Boyne, Barrow, Nore, Suir and Slaney were all carried out in the second half of the eighteenth century and between 1825 and 1842 the

A fly-boat, c. 1840

An early passage boat entering Harcourt Lock on the Grand Canal

Ulster Canal, linking Lough Neagh with Upper Lough Erne, was built at a cost of over a quarter of a million pounds.

Four other projects complete the picture: between 1839 and 1850 a major scheme of navigational and drainage improvement along the course of the Shannon was carried out under the supervision of the 'Commissioners for the Improvement of the River Shannon'; between 1842 and 1852 the Lough Corrib Navigation established a link between Lough Corrib and the sea at Galway; between 1847 and 1859 the Irish Board of Public Works made navigable the courses of the Upper and Lower Bann, from Portadown to Coleraine; and between 1846 and 1859 the ill-fated Ballinamore and Bally-connell Canal carried the line of the Ulster Canal south-westwards across

County Leitrim to the headwaters of the Shannon, creating a third line of inland navigation across Ireland from the east coast to the Shannon and Limerick.

Having outlined the basic chronology of canal construction let us pause for a moment and see what physical and economic factors prompted the various waterways, and to what extent the high hopes and massive expenditure of public funds which we have already noted were justified in the years which followed. For convenience here Irish canals may be considered in four groups: northern, central, western and south eastern.

In the north the over-riding factor dictating the construction of the Newry Canal was the determination of Dublin interests to tap extensive coal deposits which had recently been discovered between Dungannon and Coalisland in east Tyrone, beyond the western shore of Lough Neagh. The inland section of the Newry Navigation was constructed between 1731 and 1742 under the provisions of an Act of 1729 which had established four bodies of commissioners, one for each province, to supervise the allocation of funds resulting from duties to be levied on gold and silver plate, playing cards and on 'coaches, berlins, calashes, chaises and chairs.' These 'tillage duties'—so called because their main object was to encourage drainage and tillage throughout the country—provided the financial backing for the Newry Canal, constructed by the Irish Parliament as both a drainage conduit and a navigation channel. This canal, with fifteen locks in an over-all length of approximately eighteen miles, at first accommodated small, masted vessels, horse-drawn on the inland canal but capable of making coastwise voyages to Dublin in summer. Subsequently all cargoes were transhipped at Newry, the barges or lighters operating on the inland canal, measuring some sixty feet in length, fifteen feet in width, and with a draught of five feet two inches. With completion between 1760 and 1769 of the first ship canal, below the town, affording entry and exit to vessels of up to 150 tons burden, the port of Newry, situated at the head of an elongated and hazardous tidal estuary, advanced to a position of national importance during the second half of the eighteenth century.[2]

With the success of the Newry Canal to the south and the increasing exploitation of the coal deposits of east Tyrone, the construction of a navigation linking Belfast and the lower Lagan valley with the shores of Lough Neagh was not long delayed. The canal here was built in two sections: the 'canalisation' of the river below Lisburn, completed in 1763, and the summit

The aqueduct near Newmills, Co. Tyrone, by which Ducart carried his 'tub boat' canal over the river Torrent (1770)

level and descent to Lough Negah, not built until twenty years later.[3]

Work on the Tyrone navigation system began in 1732–3 and here again it was the prospect of having access to an extensive coalfield, with barge traffic down to Lough Neagh, south-eastwards to Newry, and coastwise shipment to Dublin, which induced the Irish Parliament to expend large sums of money over a long period. The Coalisland Canal proper was quite short and linked the Blackwater, entering Lough Neagh, with Coalisland itself, some four miles to the west. During the period of construction it was found that the ease, speed and cheapness of the coal export was being greatly handicapped by the fact that the canal basin at Coalisland lay some three miles east of the chief area of mineral workings. To combat expensive land carriage a headward extension of the Tyrone Navigation was built from the canal basin at Coalisland westward to the Drumglass collieries. This short 'tub-boat' canal is worthy of interest in that it included the sole examples in Ireland of 'inclined planes' or 'gravitational inclines', known locally as 'dry hurrys'. The construction of these inclines by the continental engineer, Daviso de Arcort (Ducart), is of particular interest and significance as they were the earliest canal inclines built in the British Isles in modern times. The inclined plane—a method of overcoming gradient on canals other than by the more normal lockage—was used in Ancient China, but apart from several examples in Renaissance Italy it had gone out of fashion. Ducart began by building timber ramps laid on the causeways of the inclined planes, the ramps being equipped with surface rollers, and in this it seems probable that he had knowledge of the *ponts aux rouleaux* of seventeenth-century continental canals, where the power required to haul a boat up the ramp was provided by great water-wheels. However, it appears that Ducart experienced considerable difficulty in providing the power necessary to pull boats up the ramps and on hearing from John Smeaton he tried to make the inclines work by counter-balancing: i.e. a loaded boat in descent was to haul up an empty one on an adjoining causeway. Despite detailed experiments on various methods of negotiating the ramps or 'hurrys' Ducart's scheme was never a great commercial success, and although complete in 1777 and in limited use in the years immediately following, the entire Coalisland-Drumglass extension was a gross mis-application of effort. Its failure had probably been realised long before its completion but it had been finished for no other reason than to prevent the prosecution of Ducart for the blatant misuse of public money.[4]

At the beginning of the nineteenth century the idea of linking the lowlands around Lough Neagh with those around Upper and Lower Erne became popular with the more progressive and enlightened landed proprietors and merchants in counties Armagh, Monaghan and Fermanagh. The forty-two-mile Ulster Canal was constructed between 1825 and 1842 by the Ulster Canal Company at a cost of over £250,000, most of this borrowed from the Exchequer Bill Loan Commissioners. At the outset engineering was in the hands of John Killaly and Thomas Telford, the latter acting in his official capacity as consultant for all schemes being carried out with funds borrowed from the Treasury, but the greater part of the canal was built after the death of both these men and was the work of Thomas Casebourne and William Cubitt.

The canal made possible through-communication by water from Belfast

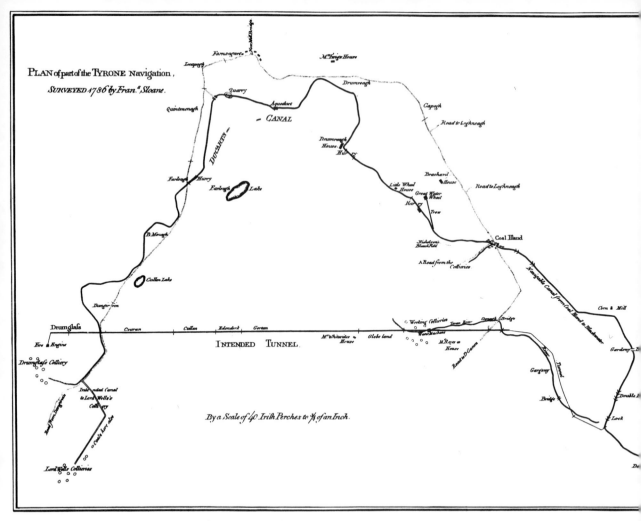

Francis Sloane's plan of part of the Tyrone navigation system, 1786, showing Ducart's Canal and an intended tunnel from the collieries at Drumglass

to Belleek, and it was hoped that a south-westerly continuation of this line of navigation across the lake-studded surface of County Leitrim to the headwaters of the Shannon would soon provide a third great line of water transit across Ireland, similar to the Grand and Royal Canals stretching westward from Dublin. This extension, the Ballinamore and Ballyconnell Canal, was not completed until 1859 and proved a dismal failure during the few years it remained open to commercial traffic.[5]

Conceived as an important 'link' navigation rather than as a major waterway in its own right, it was imperative that to succeed, the Ulster Canal should be in a position to handle a great variety of through traffic passing from the Lough Neagh basin south-westward towards the Erne lowlands and the headwaters of the Shannon. It is therefore difficult to understand why those in charge of its construction should have immediately rendered the bulk of such traffic impossible by erecting locks of insufficient width or depth to handle the normal lighter traffic from the Lagan and Newry Navigations, and from Lough Neagh. This factor, coupled with extreme scarcity of water in the western reaches towards Lough Erne, did much to nullify the engineering skill displayed by Telford in negotiating the gorge of the Blackwater at Benburb, where the canal course had to be benched into a steep-sided ravine some twenty feet above the level of the swiftly-flowing river. Besides substantial embanking and puddling, seven locks were required within a distance of less than three-quarters of a mile; the cost of this section alone, little over a mile in all, was between £17,000 and £18,000. From a total expenditure of over a quarter of a million pounds, those in control of the Ulster Canal during its relatively brief life were never able to recoup more than £500 per annum, a sum miserably short of that often required by normal maintenance and regular operational expenditure.[6]

The Grand and Royal Canals, parallel waterways traversing the heartland from east to west, enjoyed no more than moderate success in the goods and merchandise which they carried, but from the end of the eighteenth century a flourishing passenger service developed, with canal boats moving out across the Central Plain at a leisurely pace, from Dublin to the Shannon.[7] On the Grand Canal, hotels were built for the comfort of passengers at Portobello

Dublin from Blaquiere Bridge, Royal Canal

The Royal Canal harbour, Broadstone, Dublin, 1821

(Dublin), Sallins, Robertstown, Tullamore and Shannon Harbour, and regular services were introduced, boats leaving Dublin on Mondays and Thursdays, returning on Tuesdays and Fridays. The journey to Shannon Harbour—a distance of eighty miles—took eighteen hours and in 1818 the fare was a guinea for first class and 14s. for second class. In the same year the Royal Canal had four passenger boats in regular service; the journey from Dublin to Mullingar, a distance of fifty-three miles, took thirteen and a half hours, with fares 12s. 6d. and 7s. 7d. In view of the slowness of canal travel the boats were equipped with facilities for serving meals on board, and each boat carried between seventy and eighty passengers. In addition to the regular services, special journeys were made as required to Maynooth, to Mullingar Assizes, to Ballinasloe Fair, and at Easter, Whitsun and Christmas.

Contemporary accounts give us a glimpse of this new form of travel in the early nineteenth century: the following is a traveller's description of the journey on the Grand Canal, from Athy to Dublin dating from 1803:

... PRECISELY AS the clock struck one, the towing horse started, and we slipped through the water in the most delightful manner imaginable, at the rate of four miles an hour. The boat appeared to be about 35 feet long, having a raised cabin, its roof forming a deck to walk upon. The cabin was divided into a room for the principal passengers, having cushioned seats and windows in either side, and a long table in the middle, and into another room for the servants of the vessel and the pantry: the kitchen was in the steerage ... The day was very fine, and the company very respectable and pleasant. We had an excellent dinner on board, consisting of a leg of boiled mutton, a turkey, ham, vegetables, porter, and a pint of wine each, at four shillings and ten pence a head ... Our liquid road lay through very fine country, adorned with several noble seats ... We slept at Robertstown, where there is a noble inn belonging to the Canal company, and before day-light set off for Dublin, where after descending a great number of locks, and passing through a long avenue of fine elms, we arrived about ten o'clock a.m. All the regulations of these boats are excellent. I was so delighted with my canal conveyance, that if the objects which I had in view had not been so powerful, I verily think I should have spent the rest of my time in Ireland in the Athy canal boat ...[8]

Not all visitors were so easily satisfied and as the century advanced, increasing competition from mail and stage coaches prompted the introduction of 'fly-boat' services, drawn by three horses at a speed of ten m.p.h. by day and six m.p.h. by night. The journey time from Dublin to Ballinasloe was reduced to eleven hours by day, to Athy it was cut to seven and a half hours, and by 1837 the number of passengers travelling on the Grand and Royal Canals exceeded 150,000.[9] Mail and stage coaches linked up with the canal boat services and Charles Bianconi also ran connections with canal services and carried passengers from Kilbeggan to Athlone, from Ballinasloe to Galway and from Mountmellick to Birr. In the pre-railway era many people chose to travel by canal wherever possible: it was more comfortable, less tiring and

75

REGULATIONS
OF
Grand Canal Passage Boats.

RATES OF FARES AND ORDINARY,
In English Currency.

DAY BOATS, from *Dublin, Tullamore,* and *Athy,* respectively, at SEVEN o'Clock every Morning.

Stages.	Distances. From Dublin.	Fares, Between Dublin and respective Stages.		Hours of Arrival.	
		First Cabin.	Second Cabin.	From Dublin.	To Dublin.
	English Miles	S. D.	S. D.	H. M.	H. M.
Dublin, ...					8 10
Hazel-Hatch, ...	11	2 0	1 2	10 0	5 10
Sallins, ...	19	3 3	2 0	11 45	3 25
Robertstown, ...	26	4 2	2 6	1 20	{ 1 25° / 1 50† }
Rathangan, ...	34½	5 0	2 11	3 25	11 30
Monastereven, ...	41	5 6	3 3	4 55	10 0
Vicarstown, ...	48	5 6	3 3	6 40	8 15
Athy, ...	54¼	5 6	3 3	7 55	
Ticknevin, ...	33½	5 3	3 0	3 15	12 15
Edenderry Branch, ...	38	6 0	3 3	3 50	11 40
Ballybritain, ...	41	6 6	3 6	4 50	10 40
Philipstown, ...	49	7 10	4 0	6 30	9 0
Tullamore, ...	57½	9 2	4 9	8 30	
				° From Athy / † Tullamore	

NIGHT BOATS, from *Dublin,* at Two o'Clock, and from *Shannon Harbour,* at FOUR o'Clock, every Afternoon.

Stages.	Distances, From Dublin.	Fares, Between Dublin and respective Stages.		Hours of Arrival.	
		First Cabin.	Second Cabin.	From Dublin.	To Dublin.
	English Miles	S. D.	S. D.	H. M.	H. M.
Dublin, ...					10 15
Hazel-Hatch, ...	11	2 0	1 2	5 0	7 15
Sallins, ...	19	3 3	2 0	6 45	6 0
Robertstown, ...	26	4 2	2 6	8 20	4 30
Ticknevin, ...	33½	5 3	3 0	10 0	2 50
Edenderry Branch, ...	38	6 0	3 3	10 35	2 10
Ballybritain, ...	41	6 6	3 6	11 40	1 10
Philipstown, ...	49	7 10	4 0	1 25	11 25
Tullamore, ...	57½	9 2	4 9	3 30	9 5
Corrinalor, ...	65	10 2	5 4	5 55	7 10
Gillen, ...	73½	11 0	6 0	7 35	5 30
Shannon Harbour, ...	79½	12 0	6 6	9 5	

FARE—for each stage, *between Rathangan and Athy,* First Cabin, 8d...Second Cabin, 5d. Fare, in Boat between James's-street Harbour and First Lock—First Cabin, 5d...Second Cabin, 3d.

Any Passenger travelling Part of one Stage is to pay for the whole—but any Person travelling one Stage and Part of another, (the Stage between Dublin and Hazel-Hatch excepted) to pay for such Part of a Stage, 3d. per Mile for the First, and 2d. per Mile for the Second Cabin.

CHILDREN, under two Years of Age, not charged for in either Cabin—and only Half-price for any Child between that Age and ten Years.

DOGS to be paid for as Passengers.

LUGGAGE—Each First Cabin Passenger allowed to take 84 lbs. weight of Luggage, free of Charge, but not more than two hundred weight in the whole. Each Second Cabin Passenger allowed to take 28 lbs. of Luggage, free of Charge, but not more than one hundred weight in the whole. *Extra Luggage* charged at ½d. per lb. per Stage—not to exceed 1d. per lb. for any Distance. All Portmanteaus and Parcels, sufficiently small, to be stowed in the Lockers, are to be so deposited immediately on their being put on board; and no Parcel of any kind to be suffered to remain on the Tables or Seats, in either of the Cabins, under the Penalty of a severe Fine on the Boat-master. Passengers may send their Luggage to the Keepers of the Company's Luggage Offices, at Portobello Hotel and James's-street Harbour, or to the Collectors of Tolls, at their respective Stations; to whom Orders are given to pay every possible attention to them: but the Company will not be responsible for the Luggage of any Passenger. No Furniture or other bulky Articles to be admitted into the Boats.

PARCELS—are received, or delivered, at the following Places on the Canal, viz. Parcel Offices, at Portobello and James's-street Harbour, DUBLIN; the 12th Lock, Sallins, Robertstown, Rathangan, Monastereven, Vicarstown, Athy, Ticknevin, Philipstown, Tullamore, Gillen, and Shannon Harbour; and at any Lock on the Line—and are also carried by any of the Coaches, or other Conveyances, running in Connexion with the Canal. RATES—One-Halfpenny per lb. any Distance on the Canal not exceeding 26 Miles—but not less than 8d. each Parcel.

| Three Farthings | ... | ... | ... | 58 Miles | ... | 1s. 0d. | ... |
| One Penny | ... | ... | ... | exceeding 58 Miles | ... | 1s. 4d. | ... |

Parcels from the Country are delivered in Dublin, as directed, at an additional Charge of 3d. each.

No Parcel containing Gunpowder, Letters, Spirits, or having an offensive Smell, will be received. No Parcel of extraordinary Bulk, or exceeding 28 lbs. weight, admitted, when productive of any Inconvenience to Passengers. The Company will not be responsible for any Parcel exceeding Two Pounds Sterling in Value.

GENERAL REGULATIONS—No Servant in Livery to be admitted as a Passenger in the First Cabin—No more than Forty-five Passengers for the First Cabin, nor Thirty-five for the Second Cabin, to be admitted into the Boat; and should any Persons, exceeding those Numbers respectively, obtrude themselves into the Boat, the Boat-master is not on any account to proceed, until they shall have withdrawn. Any Second-Cabin Passenger remaining on Deck, after Notice from the Boat-master to withdraw, to pay as for the First Cabin. The Price of Passage, and of extra Luggage, to be paid by each Passenger on entering the Boat, or as soon as the Boat-master may demand the same: and every Person so paying, is requested to see Payment entered by the Boat-master, in his Book; which he is to produce to any Passenger who may desire to inspect it, or to enter any Observation or Complaint therein—No Person is to stand on Deck, so as to intercept the view of the Steerer—No smoking of Tobacco to be permitted in either Cabin—nor any Gaming on Sundays, under the Penalty on the Boat-master of Two Guineas for each Offence.

A private Room is provided for Ladies, to which no other Person can be admitted. There is also a private Room for Gentlemen.

Waiting Rooms for the Passengers are also provided at Portobello Hotel and James's-street Harbour, and at the Hotels or Collectors' Houses, on the Lines from Dublin to Athy and Shannon Harbour.

RATES OF ORDINARY.

FIRST CABIN.	s. d.	SECOND CABIN.	s. d.
Breakfast, with Eggs, ...	1 3	Breakfast, with an Egg, ...	0 10
Dinner, ...	2 2	Dinner, ...	1 3
Porter, per Bottle, ...	0 5	Porter, per Bottle, ...	0 5
Cider, per Bottle, ...	0 10	Cider, per Bottle, ...	0 10
Pint of Port or White Wine,	2 0	Supper, ...	1 0
Half Pint ditto, ...	1 0	Tea, or Coffee, after Dinner,	0 10
Naggin of Spirits, with Sugar,	0 10		
Half Naggin ditto, ...	0 10	*No Wine, or Spirits, to be sold in Second Cabin.*	
Tea or Coffee, after Dinner,	0 10		
Supper, ...	1 3		
Sugar, after Dinner or Supper,	0 2		

Wine, sold only in Pints, or Half-pints—and not more than one Pint to each Person—No Wine or Spirits furnished to any Child under the Age of ten Years—nor is the Allowance of Wine or Spirits to one Person, without his or her express desire, to be transferred to another.

A Naggin of Spirits, instead of Wine, or Half a Naggin of Spirits, together with Half a Pint of Wine, allowed to each Gentleman in the State Cabin, after Dinner or Supper-time; but such Allowance of Spirits not extended to Women or Children—Children from *two to ten* Years old to pay only *Half* the Rates of Ordinary—No Charge for Waiters; nor Gratuities to be accepted by the Boat-masters, Waiters, or Boatmen, on any Pretence whatever, on pain of *Dismission.*

The foregoing Regulations being intended for the general Accommodation and Convenience of the Passengers, they are requested to enter any Infringement or Non-observance thereof, in the Boat-master's Book, or to communicate the same by Letter, addressed to the Company's Secretary, at his Office, No. 49½, William-street, Dublin.

BY ORDER,

EDWARD LAWSON.

5th January, 1826.

more reliable than road travel, and though the introduction of faster services destroyed the economic justification for the impressive company hotels there was more than a suggestion of adventure in embarking on a canal journey across the Bog of Allen towards the western sea.

By 1840, however, we are on the eve of the railway age and within ten years it was as unthinkable to travel by canal boat as it had been less than a century previously. Despite the inherent attractions of leisurely canal travel the practical advantages of even the most rudimentary form of rail transport over the canal boat may be seen from this description written in 1845:

... IT IS LONG and narrow; covered in as we see it; and there are two divisions for different classes of passengers. As a mode of travelling it is exceedingly inconvenient; there is scarcely space to turn in the confined cabin; and an outside 'berth' for more than one is impossible. The guide, or guard, takes his stand at the bow of the boat, and a helmsman controls its motions. It proceeds at a very rapid pace—about seven Irish miles an hour—drawn by two or three horses, who are made to gallop all the way. There is a more cumbrous vessel, called a 'night boat', which travels at a much slower rate—about four miles an hour—and always at night. It is large, awkward, and lumbering, and is chiefly used by the peasantry on account of its cheapness ...[10]

By 1850 passenger canal traffic was dead.

The extensive navigation works carried out on the Shannon between 1839 and 1850 were never rewarded by a commensurate return in commercial traffic in goods or passengers. Within three years of opening, the number of passengers being carried annually had dropped from over 16,000 to less than 11,000, and while the entire scheme was of great benefit in providing employment for a destitute peasantry during the troubled years of the Famine, and in facilitating the construction of railways throughout the area, the commercial importance of the river declined throughout the rest of the century, from 121,702 tons carried in 1847 to 41,720 tons in 1885. By the end of the century the annual tonnage again exceeded 80,000 but this increase was a reflection more of the increase of trade on the Grand Canal than of that on the Shannon

The opening of the Eglinton Canal, 1852

itself. One of the chief difficulties in establishing successful commercial traffic on the Shannon was that the canal barges plying from Dublin were not suitable for the heavy weather often encountered on the exposed waters of the river and its lakes. This meant that both cargo and passengers had to be transhipped at Shannon Harbour, a costly and time-wasting break, especially in the transport of heavy merchandise. Commercial barge traffic continued until 1960 when it was withdrawn by C.I.E.: the river remains open for pleasure traffic and the value of the navigation in this respect is now receiving official recognition.[11]

A flow-line diagram of northern canal traffic, 1836, 1910, 1940

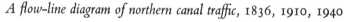

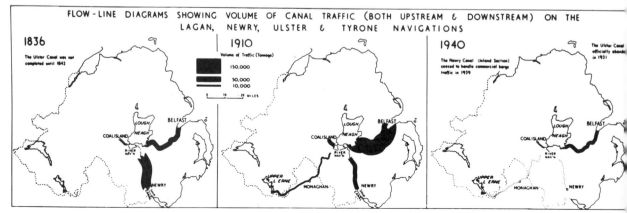

FLOW-LINE DIAGRAMS SHOWING VOLUME OF CANAL TRAFFIC (BOTH UPSTREAM & DOWNSTREAM) ON THE LAGAN, NEWRY, ULSTER & TYRONE NAVIGATIONS

So far as passenger traffic on the Shannon is concerned, there is no lack of descriptive documentation as many visitors from both Britain and overseas making the 'Grand Tour' in the mid-nineteenth century committed their experiences to print on return. The following extract from an account of a journey down the river, written in 1842 by a German visitor, affords both description and comment:

. . . AS THERE ARE no railroads in Ireland, with the exception of two miniature ones . . . the canals which traverse the country are much used for travelling, and boats, generally full to overflowing, ply regularly from and to Dublin. The boats, like the *treckschuits* in Holland, are drawn by horses that move along at a smart trot . . . It was on a beautiful day that I embarked to descend the Shannon. Flowing out of a lake, and forming several other lakes in its progress, the water is extremely clear and beautiful . . . The most remarkable part of our cargo consisted in a consignment of oxen and cows from Hamburg . . . Beyond Killaloe we come again to rocks and whirlpools, and as the canal was not yet finished (by means of which this part of the river is to be avoided) we had the amusement of landing bag and baggage, and proceeding with jaunting cars to the spot where it was possible to embark for Limerick. The captain of the steamer and his mates shipped themselves on the backs of some cantering nags and rattled away in front as commanders and escort to the caravan. At the end of a few miles we embarked again, but this time in a long canal boat drawn by a

Steam lighter 'Ulster' at Merchants' Quay, Newry, c. 1893. This type of shallow-draught vessel plied regularly between Newry and Portadown towards the end of the nineteenth century.

Sand barges at Queen's Bridge, Belfast, c. 1890. There was for many years substantial down-stream traffic in sand and gravel from Lough Neagh to Belfast, along the Lagan Navigation.

couple of horses. All this sounds rather wild and Irish; in England such a variegated mode of transport is scarcely to be found . . .[12]

In the south east flour-milling, malting, brewing and distilling at towns such as Clonmel, New Ross and Carrick-on-Suir were of considerable importance in the early nineteenth century and water traffic in flour, wheat, oats, barley, butter, lard, bacon, coal, turf and timber was for many years of substantial proportions. Gradually, however, as on the Grand and Royal Canals, the slowness of canal transport proved too great a disadvantage in the pace of modern commerce and the lack of heavy and sustained mineral traffic, and lack of a diversified flow of industrial products and raw materials— combined with the physical difficulties confronting barge traffic in canalised river courses—have led to the virtual disappearance of commercial traffic.

Successful elsewhere, canals were constructed in Ireland simply because it was thought that such developments would create and stimulate traffic, as they had done in Great Britain, and in more than one instance merely to provide employment for an impoverished local population. Numerous lakes and navigable rivers often facilitated canal engineering but this was not sufficient to outweigh an overall lack of justification in the cultural environment. The majority of the lines of navigation were never able to command a traffic volume of anything like the dimensions required for commercial stability, and with the rapid growth of the railways in the mid-nineteenth century their difficulties were further accentuated.

For well over a hundred years canals such as the Newry and Lagan enjoyed a moderate degree of success, carrying agricultural produce and local manufactures to the ports for export or further processing, and distributing fuel, grain and raw materials over wide areas round the shores of Lough Neagh or along the river valleys radiating from it. Passenger traffic on the Grand and Royal Canals flourished for a short time, a transient phase in the development of internal transport and communication in Ireland, but neither here nor in the south east of the country was the traffic provided by industries based essentially on agriculture sufficient to sustain the canals and river navigations in the face of competition from rail and road transport.

As a commercial transport medium the canals are finished, but this is not to say that those which remain should be abandoned or tastelessly adapted to other uses without due consideration of the amenity potential which some of them offer in the modern concept of expanding leisure.

Lighters and steam tugs at Portadown bridge, c. 1925

6 Bianconi and his Cars

Thomas P. O'Neill

CARLO BIANCONI was born at Tregolo, a village near Como in northern Italy in 1786. He was sixteen years of age when taken to Ireland by a fellow-countryman, Andrea Faroni, in 1802. Georgian Dublin was just beginning to decline but there was plenty of scope for the sellers of cheap prints. Engravings of a topical kind, satires on fashions and on politics, were a craze and Irish publishers were not too chary about copying from well-known English artists such as Rowlandson and Gillray. Napoleon was the caricaturists' main political butt while the doings of the 10th Hussars provided scope for artists who depicted tight-laced dandies and loose-living women. Books of caricatures and satirical engravings were to be had from publishers like Sidebotham, McCleary, Le Pettit and del Vecchio in Dublin, not only to buy but also to rent as the centrepiece for an evening's entertainment in the drawing rooms of the Georgians.

There was hope for the pedlar of these goods in an age when illustration was still in its infancy. The big houses throughout Ireland provided a steady market for this type of engraving and also for the reproduction of works of art which were part of the print seller's stock-in-trade. Poorer people purchased less ambitious religious prints. Charles Bianconi, as his name was to be rendered in Ireland, was placed in lodgings in Temple Bar near Essex Bridge in Dublin and first learned to cast cheap leaden picture frames from a stone mould. Then he was sent on to the streets of the city, not knowing a word of the language, to sell his wares. Later he was sent down the country to Wexford and Waterford and tramped the countryside with a box of framed prints on his back. He wrote long afterwards, 'I knew neither discouragement

82

nor fatigue, for I felt that I had set to work to become a great man'. There must have been an element of hindsight in this view for, at the time, the print pedlar must have appeared doomed to tramp on foot through life; to rise to having a horse of his own for carrying himself and his wares must have been the height of his early hopes. Ambition was very strong, however, and when it was backed by charm it opened many doors. The 'curly-headed Italian boy' made friends with priests and with people in the south along the valley of the Suir. He was welcomed in the houses of landed families and of professional people as well as among the poor.

He decided that if he were to improve his position he must leave the roads and take on the dignity of a shop-keeper. This he did in 1806 when he opened for business in Carrick-on-Suir as a carver and gilder. Later he moved to Waterford for a couple of years and finally established himself in Clonmel. Bianconi was not an expert gilder but he was an efficient and astute business-man. He added mirrors imported direct from London to his stock, and employed skilled assistants to carve and gild frames for them and for his pictures. In the meantime he travelled the country soliciting orders and delivering goods. It was a measure of his self-assurance that, on limited capital, he employed assistants while devoting himself to the tasks to which he was best suited. He had at all times an eye to business and he was soon engaged in the bullion trade, the buying of gold to pay the armies engaged in the last phases of the struggle against Napoleon.

The collecting of golden guineas was to prove a profitable side-line to gilding frames and at the end of the Napoleonic wars Bianconi was in a position to take advantage of such opportunities as might present themselves. Tramping Irish roads had opened his eyes to the possibilities of a cheap transport system. The battle of Waterloo was fought in June 1815; the following month Charles Bianconi launched the enterprise which was to make his name and his fortune. He established a scheduled car service to run to a set time-table. The route chosen, the road between Clonmel and Cahir, was short, a distance of only ten miles. When in later life Bianconi was asked why he chose to make his first venture between Clonmel and Cahir instead of linking Clonmel with more populous and prosperous towns in the district he had a simple answer: Carrick-on-Suir and Cashel were just that little bit too far to allow a horse to make the journey to and fro in a single day. He was able to start his Cahir-Clonmel service with one horse and car. He also

saw that while there were boats on the river to Carrick-on-Suir and the mail
coach to Dublin which went through Cashel, there was no transport linking
Clonmel with Cahir. Bianconi, it is said, found that his first venture was not
as successful as he had hoped. People were used to trudging on foot and money
was more valuable to most of them than time. But when he decided to run
an opposition car which was not known to be his, on the same road, the
excitement of competition attracted attention and soon both cars were filled
each day.

Once established the project prospered. Before the end of 1815 Bianconi
had extended his service to link Clonmel and Limerick and had also opened a
regular line from Clonmel to Thurles. The following year he had a car service
between Clonmel and Waterford in operation. By 1819 he had established
his cars on the roads between Waterford, New Ross, Enniscorthy and Wex-

ford. Two years later he had opened a line to Cork. By 1825 his cars were covering over a thousand miles of roads each day, linking the principal towns of south Leinster and east Munster. Bianconi's cars were an established feature of Irish transport by this time.

Expansion was to continue through the next couple of decades. Bianconi was running cars to Athlone, Longford and Ballinasloe by 1831 and by 1834 he had cars running west to Tralee and through Connacht as far north as Sligo. On 8 September 1832 the *Dublin Penny Journal* had a laudatory article on the enterprise of the Italian who had by this time over 300 horses and 120 employees. His cars were travelling some 1,800 miles a day: 'Before Mr Bianconi established his cars, the travelling vehicles in use were only four-horse coaches, confined to what are termed the mail coach roads, and the fares were too high for the humbler class of farmers and tradesmen, whose business often calls them from home.'

The most noteworthy aspect of the business which Bianconi was building up was that it was built not along the main arteries of traffic, but crossing them. Most of the public transport which existed in Ireland up to his time was Dublin orientated. It linked the provinces with the metropolis but did not help travel between Irish provincial towns. It is possible to make a comparison between the routes followed by Bianconi's cars in 1835 and those of the largest coaching establishment in the country, that of Messrs Purcell and Company of Dublin. Almost all of the services of the latter radiated out from Dublin. Only two of its lines linked the major towns of Munster and these were perhaps an attempt to challenge the supremacy which Bianconi had built up in that province. But the effort was ineffectual: where Purcell's lines coincided with Bianconi's the latter was carrying almost eighty per cent

of the passengers. Another firm operating at the same time, Gossons, was also centred on Dublin and sent coaches to north Leinster and to the southern counties of Ulster.

Competition was keen in travel in those years. The 1830s had seen a great growth in the development of road transport in all areas even those outside Bianconi's influence. By the early 1840s only a few of the most remote parts of Ireland were more than ten miles from some form of public transport. From Derry, for example, nine services were opened with towns in its hinterland between 1833 and 1836. Bianconi was not to extend his services into Ulster until the 1850s and then he confined himself to the west of the province with cars running as far north as Letterkenny. Throughout the country, he often faced local challenges. When he entered many an area he found services already being run by small coaching houses and he put many of them out of business. This he did by having a more competitive organisation and better equipment. A diarist in the 1840s wrote of one of these rival car-owners, one McCarthy of Kanturk: 'His cars in shape and size resemble Bianconi's, but here the comparison ends, as McCarthy's horses are poor starved hacks, whereas those of Bianconi are fine, well-fed and strong.'

Bianconi set great store by his horses. A tourist who interviewed him recorded: 'He attributes the regularity with which he carries on his extensive establishment to the high price he gives for his horses (sometimes it is over forty pounds), which enables him to keep constantly a capital supply.'

He was assisted initially by the fact that he started business as the Napoleonic wars ended, for peace made available a great number of first-class horses bred for the army. There was not much competition for their purchase at the time and so Bianconi was able to avail of the opportunity to get together strong horses which were a valuable asset in building up his business. Also he was careful not to overwork them. In general his cars did not run on Sundays, partly because there were few passengers on the Sabbath but also because he found that the day of rest helped his horses to work better on the other days of the week. He also laid down strict rules as to the ration of oats, hay and straw for bedding allowed to each horse and while he would surcharge any agent who might inadvertently be too generous, he also took precautions to see that the horses were not short-rationed. For example no groom's wife was allowed to keep hens lest she fatten them on Bianconi's oats at the expense of the horses. The little Italian was proud of his teams of horses. Each horse had a name and it was claimed that the owner knew each one of them. The arrival of the horses at a starting point such as Cummin's Hotel in Waterford was always an attraction to admirers of horse-flesh. The fine greys which

were always associated with the Clonmel car were in the most prominent position. One of them was a remarkable animal named Pender, reputed to be blind but guided in masterly fashion by the reins in the hand of the driver, Pat Dillon.

Indeed the drivers were as spectacular as their charges and a great deal depended on them. William Mullaly on the Waterford-Kilkenny road was one of the most popular, with a natural enthusiasm for horses. The challenge of a rival car-owner on that route afforded Mullaly many an opportunity for displaying his daring and skill. Then there was Tim Haly, commonly known by the nickname Lord Gort, whose repertoire of stories kept his passengers amused on the Clonmel to Cork line. The pay of these drivers was small for Bianconi was a careful man when it came to spending money. His car-drivers depended for a substantial portion of their income on tips paid to them by passengers, a system which the owner acknowledged by promoting his men from lines which carried less passengers, to the more lucrative ones. In fact such promotion often meant a loss in wages to the driver but it was more than compensated for by his increased income from his passengers.

Horses and drivers were important to the success of Bianconi's venture. So too were the cars he developed. Up to his time most of the road passenger traffic was carried in enclosed heavy coaches which carried extra passengers perched precariously on top. The latter paid a lesser fare than those inside the coach. Bianconi's cars were a development of the Irish jaunting car with passengers seated on each side facing the hedgerows. In between was a well in which luggage was carried, sometimes piled so high that it formed a barrier between the two rows of passengers.

As the business grew so too did the cars. They became longer and longer and soon four-wheeled vehicles were replacing two-wheeled ones. The largest of the two-wheelers were named 'Massey Dawsons' after a popular Tory landlord. These carried five persons on each side and were drawn by one horse between the shafts and another horse whose traces were fixed to a swinging bar, running alongside. When fully laden, the weight of this vehicle on a horse's back was becoming too much, especially as the heavy artillery horses of Bianconi's earlier stables were being replaced by a lighter breed. Thus Bianconi developed his four wheel cars. The longest of these were to be known as 'Finn McCools' after the legendary Irish giant, and were built to take as many as twenty passengers. These were fitted with a pole instead of shafts and the horses were tackled one at each side. If extra horses were needed they were tackled to swinging bars at the front. All his open cars were to be known affectionately as 'Bians'.

The seating on the cars was well designed to compete with the accommodation for outside passengers on the coaches. Dry, comfortable horsehair cushions were provided and in wet weather a car was never allowed to go more than two stages without changing the cushions. The cushions were laid on slats so that they would not rest in the wet. Passengers were also able to protect themselves to some extent with heavy waterproof aprons which could be drawn up to the chin.

The cars were well turned out and made of excellent materials. As his business prospered Bianconi established his own car and harness factory at Clonmel but initially he was enabled to buy his original stock of two-wheeled jaunting cars because of the imposition by the government of a carriage tax. As a consequence many people in moderate circumstances gave up their cars to Bianconi at reasonable prices and swelled the numbers who were to become his passengers. While he bought up a few existing coaching firms and in some instances, kept their coaches running, his open cars remained the main basis for his business. On less busy routes he kept two-wheeled cars running until he finally disposed of his business, but the four-wheelers carried most of the traffic by then.

The 'Bians' were well painted, with yellow and crimson as the preponderating colours. On the backs of every car the names of the larger towns which Bianconi cars served were painted in gold on a red ground. They were an advertisement for the service, for the owner was a man with a remarkable ability for advertising in subtle ways. He succeeded in selling his service to the public. He made it fashionable to travel on a 'Bian'. While class distinction might prevent people from travelling outside on a coach there was no such

social stigma attaching to doing so on a 'Finn McCool' or a 'Massey Dawson'. Hotels were proud to boast in their advertisements, as did Kelly's Hotel in Roundstone: 'Bianconi's well appointed cars run between Galway and Roundstone daily'. Bianconi won the praise of tourists such as the Halls in 1840 for the service which he provided. They wrote 'that he has done more to improve the condition of the peasantry and the country than any other person of our age'. It was a claim which was to be made time after time on his behalf by his contemporaries.

His cars were of course to be seen everywhere in the south and west of Ireland. Sir Francis Head, the Tory propagandist who toured Ireland in a fortnight in 1852, and thus got the name Galloping Head, halted long enough near Oughterard to describe what he called 'one of Bianconi's jovial and well appointed cars'.

ON ONE SIDE, [he wrote,] sat very comfortably together, like a couple of hooded crows on a rail, two fine ruddy, powerful looking priests; next to them two English tourist ladies; then, of course, two tourist young gentlemen; and on the opposite bench, back to back to priests, ladies and Co. half a dozen more of her Majesty's subjects, all evidently in search of the picturesque.

Passengers, however, were not always so orderly. The German traveller, Kohl, had complained: 'These cars can carry an undefined number of passengers, for if the side seats are full they sit on each other's laps; or if one or two are in haste they may either stretch themselves lengthways among the luggage between the backs of the two rows of passengers, or hung on to the car in some other way'.

The English author, William Makepeace Thackeray, in 1842 also found some difficulty when travelling on the Bianconi car between Killarney and Tralee. He had tried to reserve a seat by placing his coat upon it but found that another passenger took the seat. The cars would be very comfortable conveyances, he commented, 'if the booking officers would only receive as many persons as the car would hold, and not have too many on the seats'. On this occasion he succeeded in regaining his seat by threatening to remove his luggage and take a hired post chaise instead. The extra passenger had to stretch himself uncomfortably on top of the luggage.

Even though selling prints was no longer his business and his Clonmel shop was already shut, Bianconi saw the advertising value of coloured prints of his cars. When the son of an artist friend, a young man ambitiously christened Michael Angelo Hayes, produced sketches of 'Bians' setting out from the nerve centre of the whole Bianconi system, Hearn's Hotel in Clonmel, and at various points on the road, the former print seller was interested. He persuaded Ackerman of London to engrave a set of half a dozen plates depicting 'Car-Travelling in the South of Ireland, 1836'. The pictures were well chosen to

A car to Killarney

Long cars at Gorey, Co. Wexford in the 1880s

attract the traveller. Bianconi had, with an eye to business, rejected a sketch depicting travellers drenched in torrential rain which each appeared effectively to pour down the neck of his neighbour with an umbrella. It was perhaps a little too truthful. The prints were copied into the *Illustrated London News* in 1845 and were reprinted a decade later with the date 1836 changed to 1856.

It is not too difficult to see the reasons behind the success of Bianconi's business. He provided a service for which there was a growing demand. Roads were improving in Ireland especially after the Board of Works was founded in 1830, but over many of them there was no regular transport. He filled a need, especially in the south and west where the distances between the coach routes radiating from Dublin left large tracts of the country unserved by public transport.

It has often been stated that he brought travel within the reach of the poor. This is not true: rather he served a middle-class. While his fares were cheap by comparison with those travelling inside coaches, they were still beyond the reach of many an Irishman. While one penny farthing a mile may seem cheap nowadays, a journey of six miles in pre-famine Ireland might cost more than a full day's wages to a labourer who earned but 6d or 8d a day. Not all of Bianconi's fares were as cheap as that but they were reasonable by comparison with his competitors. He kept his running costs low by a careful attention to administrative detail. He established a strict accounting system in all aspects of his business and he personally carefully checked waybills and returns filled in by agents and employees. Indeed he often said that he had no time to read anything but waybills which perhaps justifies Newman's cutting remark when Bianconi was appointed a trustee of the Catholic University: 'a gentleman well read in waybills I presume'. He also instituted a system of control by engaging inspectors who were, in fact, spies to travel and report on anything untoward which they might notice, for Bianconi was nobody's fool.

He had great business acumen. Not a single one of the lines of road on which his cars travelled in the first twenty years of his entry into the car business had to be abandoned by him as uneconomic until the coming of the railways. Then he showed his adaptability. Instead of fighting the railways as a competitor he adapted his services to them and even invested in them. His cars became 'feeders' to the trains much as they had been initially to mail-coach routes, and were to continue to do so until he sold off his business to his own agents in various districts in 1866 and retired from business. The son who would have succeeded him had predeceased him and so the business was broken up. In 1861 'Bians' were still travelling over 4,000 miles of Irish roads daily and about 900 horses were still in use. While the trains had almost completely wiped out the coach services radiating from Dublin Bianconi had succeeded in accommodating himself to the new challenge. He saw the need for services to complement the railways and carry passengers to and from stations. This was a need which was always to exist for despite the railway expansion they never penetrated the whole of Ireland. Even after Bianconi had sold his business, and even after his death in 1875, 'Bians' were to continue to run on Irish roads until replaced by omnibuses.

Much of Bianconi's success depended on the regularity of the services which he provided. It was this which won him the contracts for carrying mails which gave him an advantage over rival car owners. From the beginning, even on the Clonmel-Cahir route, he had made a bargain to carry mails for the local postmaster. Subsequently he became a contractor to several postmasters for carrying their mail, and when in 1830 the Post Office decided to make direct deals with car owners, Bianconi was able to win substantial contracts for

Charles Bianconi

carrying mail. These were a cushion against competition while his service resulted in a substantial improvement in postal communication.

From being a little Italian print seller, Bianconi had risen to being a national institution. His son was to marry Daniel O'Connell's granddaughter and his daughter was to marry O'Connell's nephew. By the 1840s he was a wealthy and successful man whose worth was recognised by being chosen as Mayor of the town of his adoption, Clonmel. He had built up his business by ploughing his profits back into it. By 1846 he was able to become a landed proprietor, the aim of many a businessman of the period. For £22,000 he bought an estate of over 1,000 acres at Longfield near Gould's Cross in County Tipperary. It was the first of his purchases of land. He was to buy a further 6,000 acres before he died. Perhaps it was the prevailing feeling that ownership of land made one a gentleman which drove the Italian immigrant to spend his money so. Even if it were he was never to lose touch with reality. When choosing a title for his projected autobiography he said that it should be called simply, *Bianconi, Carman*. That is what he is remembered as—a man who opened up the roads of Ireland on a massive scale.

The contribution of Charles Bianconi to Irish communications was made in an era which saw far-reaching changes. These were to affect the social, economic and administrative spheres of Irish life for, with improved transport, the power of central authority was to extend into the most inaccessible corners of Ireland. In Bianconi's time governments were better informed about all parts of the country than they had ever been before and the pattern of Irish life was to change under the impact of outside influences which he helped to bring to bear in localities previously isolated.

7 The Transport Revolution: The Coming of the Railways

Kevin B. Nowlan

THERE were many earlier experiments in the use of railways than the Stockton and Darlington line which began operations in 1825, but it was the first to secure parliamentary authority to convey both passengers and freight by steam locomotive power. The commercial possibilities of steam locomotives were soon recognised in Great Britain, the pioneer land in railway development, and at an early date, too, interest was shown in railway schemes in Ireland. Indeed as early as 1825 efforts were made to promote railways in Ireland, but it was not until December 1834 that the first Irish railway was opened for traffic. It was the short Dublin and Kingstown Railway which was extended, on the curious atmospheric principle, to Dalkey in 1844. The construction of this essentially suburban line did much to help open up the coastal area southwards from Dublin for residential development. Though there was some criticism of the economic value of the project at the beginning, by the mid 1840s it was already proving its economic and social value. In the year ending March 1846, for example, some 2,348,613 passengers were carried between Dublin and what was then Kingstown, and the company was able to pay as high a dividend as ten per cent. But despite the success of the Dublin and Kingstown line, railways only came slowly to Ireland.

The Dublin and Kingstown line had been opened in 1834. It was not until 1842 that the second line came into operation: it was the Ulster Railway from Belfast to Lisburn and Portadown. The early phase of railway development then, was concentrated in the Dublin area and in the immediate hinterland to the west and south of Belfast. Elsewhere in Ireland road and canal transport continued to dominate the system of internal communications.

Though we now know that the periods of heaviest investment in railways in Ireland were much the same as in Britain, the scale and intensity of railway investment and development was much less in Ireland than in the neighbouring island. This situation of course reflected the different patterns of economic growth in the two countries. Britain with its great resources of coal and iron and its strong capital position was experiencing that rough, exciting expansion of industrial production which we call the Industrial Revolution. Ireland in contrast had only very limited resources in terms of industrial power and, outside a restricted area in the north east, the country did not experience an industrial revolution to any significant extent. The need for cheaper and more efficient means of transport was a great stimulus to railway expansion in Britain. This kind of material pressure was absent in Ireland and the position here was made no easier by the widespread poverty in the country, the unsatisfactory relations between landlords and tenants in many areas and the low rate of capital investment in Irish agriculture in the first half of the nineteenth century.

As well it would seem that the ordinary Irish investor was cautious about putting his money into risk investments at home. This was a situation which complicated the task of raising funds for Irish railway construction. Yet it has

The opening of the Dublin & Kingstown Railway

The Dublin and Kingstown Railway, showing the first, second, third and fourth class carriages drawn by the locomotive Hibernia

been calculated that some £12·5 million was invested in Irish railways between 1831 and 1852, some ninety per cent coming from private sources and the balance from United Kingdom Government loans. It is difficult to determine the countries of origin of the private investments, but the funds appear to have been contributed in about equal shares by Britain and Ireland, with the initial risk capital in some cases coming from British investors.

Despite the obstacles, however, railways did come to Ireland and the contrast between the mileage at the beginning of the 1840s and at the end of the decade was to be a quite impressive one. In 1842 there was a total of only $31\frac{1}{4}$ miles of railway in Ireland. By 1850 a total of 700 miles of railway was open or under construction. The pattern of railway development varied from state to state. In some European countries where, perhaps, liberal economic theories had not taken so deep a root as in Britain, governments came to play an active role in the building and financing of railways. In Britain parliament was content merely to impose certain regulations on the railway promoters and to lay down the conditions under which approved lines could acquire land for railway purposes. The financing of the railways was left to the private capitalists and though legislative action was taken to limit the number of lines serving a region, a considerable amount of scope was left for competition between the companies.

In Ireland with its more limited financial and economic resources, it was possible to question the utility to the country of the rather 'hit or miss' character of British railway development. Following some unwise railway speculation in 1835–6, the British government set up the famous Drummond Commission to report on a suitable system of railways for Ireland. The final report of the Commission is a remarkable document, far ahead of its time in its examination of the social implications of transport and in its assessment of the volume and flow of traffic throughout the country. The Commission's practical influence on transport policies remained, however, very slight. The Commissioners considered that in the light of Ireland's limited resources, the best interests of the community would be served not by rival lines but 'by a well-combined and judicious system of railways, in which the joint traffic of many places and districts should be made to pass to a great extent over one common line, and where the greatest general accommodation should be attained at the smallest outlay.' It was also suggested by the Commissioners that with local guarantees the Government might finance, where necessary, the construction of such a systematic scheme of Irish railways. However, this

Diagram of Hibernia's engine

LOCOMOTIVE ENGINE—DUBLIN AND KINSTOWN RAILWAY

A section of the Dublin–Kingstown railway, 1834

'planned' approach was not adopted though, especially under the Peel and Russell administrations, advances were made in the 1840s to help the railway companies to complete certain lines.

Private enterprise, subject to a measure of parliamentary control as in Britain, gave Ireland its railway system. And the struggles between rival promoters to obtain parliamentary permission for their schemes often led to difficult and confused situations. The period of railway mania, as it is often called, in the mid-1840s influenced Ireland as well as Britain. During this time there were actually three rival projects for the six miles between Cork and Passage and five schemes contended for the short run between Cork and Fermoy. In 1845, some twenty-six of the forty-seven proposals that reached parliament were competing schemes.

These projects, often involving considerable variations in routes, sometimes led to bitter conflicts. The issue of whether the line northwards from Dublin should follow a coastal or an inland route was a much debated topic with considerable financial interests involved. Again, a particularly tangled struggle developed over the route to the Shannon and ultimately to the west between the Midland Railway and the powerful Great Southern and Western, which was only really resolved when the Government brought pressure to bear on the Midland to complete a line to Galway in 1851. Not surprisingly there were many railway companies which only existed on paper and there were schemes too, which bordered on fantasy. But the railways were eventually built and the way in which the state made loans-in-aid did help to maintain some limited control over the conflicting ambitions of investors. Though the state's share in the financing of the Irish railways was relatively small, it did advance some £1,180,000 to the Irish railway companies in the period between 1849 and 1854.

Despite the rivalries, personal recriminations and disputes with landowners about compensation claims as well as the grim impact of the Great Famine, railway construction continued and the pace of development quickened. In 1844 only sixty-five miles of line had been opened. By 1848 the figure had risen to slightly over 361 miles. Some pattern of development could now be traced. The short lines out of Dublin and Belfast were being lengthened and more ambitious lines were appearing on the map. Already by 1844 Dublin and Drogheda had been linked by rail and this line was to be extended soon by a branch to Howth. The Ulster Railway reached Armagh in 1848 and in the same year Belfast and Ballymena, and Belfast and Holywood were provided with railway connections. Part of the Cork and Bandon line was opened in 1849. But for the whole south of Ireland the most important railway and one involving a very substantial investment was the Great Southern and Western which finally linked Dublin and Cork in 1849. The story of the construction of a railway between Dublin and Belfast was more complicated and the project was also troubled by technical difficulties. The barrier of the Boyne remained a problem which was only finally resolved by the construction of a temporary bridge in 1853, and a permanent one in 1855. Another line worked its way down the Foyle Valley from Derry, thus opening up the western part of Ulster. As we have seen, the Dublin to Galway line was completed by 1851.

A railway map of the year 1852 shows that the basic structure of the Irish railways system had been created by then except for the routes to the north

GSWR engine built 1846-48 and withdrawn in 1875

west of Connacht and to Wexford. Dublin was linked to Cork, with a
connection to Limerick and the Great Southern and Western also served
Carlow and Kilkenny. Cork was joined to Bandon; a number of short lines
radiated out from Belfast while the Ulster Railway, in conjunction with other
companies, provided communications with Dublin. Within a decade a whole
new system of transport had been established and its influence on social
patterns and on the national economy was destined to be considerable.

The railways, as we have seen, were largely financed by private capital,
British and Irish. Some companies were to prove more profitable than others
and the men who promoted the schemes had the virtues and vices of a rather
raw period of industrial change in the nineteenth century. Most of the railway
promoters are forgotten, but some few deserve to be remembered such as the
remarkable Carlow man, William Dargan, the king of Irish railway contractors. He not merely built railways but with considerable astuteness
invested his money in railway companies. He began as a man of modest
means, but he was to show that even in the Ireland of the 1840s and 1850s it
was possible to make a very substantial fortune. There were some outstanding
Irish railway engineers too such as John MacNeill; it is obvious that British

engineers and contractors did not dominate Irish railway construction. On another level, the extensive works involved in building the railways and then the servicing of the trains and stations involved a large labour force. It has been estimated that the railway companies paid out some £4,000,000 in wages between 1845 and 1850. Not enough, it is true, to alter the tragic unbalance in Irish society, but a new source of employment and income for the people.

Railway construction was not seen by the British Government as an effective form of famine relief. In 1847 the Prime Minister, Lord John Russell, claimed that only about twenty-five per cent of the wages would go to un-skilled labour—the section most in need of help during the Famine. And he added that the companies would inevitably seek out the stronger workers rather than the weak and old. Public money, he argued, could be better spent on more conventional forms of famine relief. He therefore rejected the ambitious proposal put forward in parliament by the ultra-conservative leader, Lord George Bentinck, that some £16 million should be advanced to the Irish railways by the Treasury. As this proposal was rejected we can never know what its effect on the Irish economy might have been. But we do know that the more modest government advances, especially one of £620,000 during the actual famine period, did help the railway at a critical time when funds were short and when the Great Famine had seriously depressed the whole economy.

The Irish railways in the late 1840s and the opening years of the 1850s had their special problems which reflected the general weakness of the Irish economy, in a time of famine associated with a serious breakdown in the Irish agrarian system. Yet despite the difficulties, the Irish railway companies enjoyed certain advantages over the British undertakings. It was much cheaper to build railways in Ireland than in a prosperous, industrial country where land values were high. Wages too were significantly lower in Ireland. The result was that the Irish companies by the mid-1850s were in many cases able to pay good dividends although the volume of traffic was so much less than in Great Britain. Low construction costs naturally helped the railways but of course they would never have become the success they did were it not for the fact that railways were more than just an improvement on existing means of communication. The railways represented a fundamental revolution in communications because they employed a new source of power—steam power—the great provider of energy for a whole new industrial age.

In earlier chapters the changes that had taken place in the forms of transport over the centuries have been outlined. By the eve of the railway age, I think it is fair to say that within the limitations of horse and canal transport and the economic resources of the country, Ireland had a better transport system than we might have expected, at least in the eastern half of the island. The roads were generally described as good, much to the surprise of some travellers accustomed to the English roads which had to carry so much more heavy traffic. Thanks to the initiative of Charles Bianconi there existed a reliable and reasonably priced car service running to a published time table. The coaches too, improved their times quite significantly in the opening decades of the nineteenth century, so that by 1844 the day mail coach between Dublin and Belfast took about twelve hours compared with about fifteen hours in 1815.

The canals and river navigations helped to overcome the problem of the carriage of bulk commodities such as building materials, fuel and farm products but canal transport for passengers was slow and the actual area served by the commercial waterways was limited. Another inhibiting factor in the pre-railway era was the rather high cost of travel. For example in 1824 it cost 8s. 4d. to travel as an inside passenger on a coach from Dublin to Carlow, and if he was prepared to experience both the weather and the landscape, a passenger could take an outside seat on the roof, and pay 5s. The cheaper Bianconi cars helped to widen the market for public transport, but at a time when a labourer would be lucky to earn a shilling per day and many small farmers were hardly much better off, it is evident that the use of public transport was confined to a relatively limited section of the community.

The cost of the upkeep of coaches and cars was high. Many horses and staging posts were needed and obviously only small numbers could be carried in any one vehicle. The railways were to make some radical changes both in the economics of transport and in the social patterns of travel.

Possibly the most striking change that the railways brought about in the mid-nineteenth century was to speed up travel in a quite spectacular way. A rate of nine miles per hour was considered a smart average for a mail coach. The steam locomotives hauling a much heavier load could easily outpace both the canal flyboats and the coach. The advantages of rail transport had been recognised even before the completion of the main lines. In the 1840s we find the railways often working in close co-operation with the coach services rather than in competition with them. As a result the savings in time on the mail routes were often impressive. In 1844 the Dublin to Belfast day mail coach took, as we have seen, just under twelve hours to make the journey. By using the new railway from Dublin to Drogheda, the time taken for the Belfast journey was reduced to ten hours. But the true measure of what the railways meant in terms of speed can be seen when we turn to the timetables of the Dublin–Belfast line after the railway link had been finally completed between the two cities. In 1857 the day mail train took only five hours and twenty minutes for a journey which had taken almost double the time ten years previously and considerably longer a few years earlier still. The same story can be repeated in relation to other lines. As late as 1847, it took almost nineteen hours to travel from Dublin to Cork, although the railway was actually used as far as its temporary terminus at Athy. With the completion of the Dublin–Cork railway, the situation was dramatically altered; in 1850 the

MGW engine built in 1851

Galway terminus, 1854

same journey could be completed in just under eleven hours, and with technical improvements such times were to be cut still further.

The time factor was only one aspect of the great transport revolution. Railways also represented an important saving in transport costs despite the heavy capital investment in land, permanent ways and rolling stock. Trains could haul heavier pay loads than road vehicles. It was a case of large-scale operations bringing with them savings and more efficient methods.

For the traveller the savings could be very substantial. In 1857 the first class train fare from Dublin to Belfast was just 18s. 6d. compared to 27s. 6d. on the mail coach not so many years earlier. For an outside seat on the mail coach the fare had been 15s. With the trains, the traveller of more modest means had the choice between second class at 14s. 6d. or third class at 9s. 4d. The same pattern of low costs could be seen in other ways too. The cost per mile for example, on the Cork and Bandon Railway in 1850 was less than a penny third class, and on the Dublin and Belfast Junction Railway, the third class rate was just one penny. Rates of this kind made travel possible for more and more people. The old barriers to mobility were being broken down. By the 1850s travel had become more comfortable, cheaper and faster than ever before. It is therefore not surprising to find that in the year 1859 the Irish railways carried over 9,400,000 passengers. Some railways operators, it is true, were not at first enthusiastic about carrying third-class passengers, so that parliament had to intervene. By the Railway Regulation Act of 1844, it was provided that at least one train daily would have to be run on each line

106

for third-class passengers at a fare rate not in excess of a penny per mile. The railways were destined to serve, as their very nature demanded, not the needs of a small category of travellers, but the requirements of mass travel.

Away from the limited areas served by the canals and navigations the overland transport of goods was a costly and time-consuming business. The railways also made great changes in the carriage of freight and they helped, too, to open up parts of the country which, through isolation, had not been able to share fully in the market economy. The problems involved in the pre-railway age are well illustrated by the fact that it could take four to five days to convey bulk goods overland from Galway to Dublin. In 1851 the train took only ten hours. Some of the same conditions applied to many of the areas which were to be traversed by the Great Southern lines. A Board of Works engineer, commenting on the value of building such a railway, could say in 1847 that 'for the general exchange of commodities, the interior of this part of Ireland is virtually more remote than India or America.' His comment was no doubt an exaggeration, but it makes clear the difficulties facing traders away from the canals and seaports in the pre-railway period.

The railways did not bring with them to Ireland a phase of more intensive industrial development. The scale of railway building though substantial was not such as to alter significantly the basic structure of the Irish economy. The railways, however, did help to increase the mobility of labour, to extend the market areas of the cities and towns and to facilitate the transport of agricultural produce and livestock even from remote areas. As well, the growth of suburban districts was stimulated by the presence of railway services, as for example, along the route of the Dublin and Kingstown Railway. But railways had other implications too, for people living in the 1840s and 1850s.

Metropolitan Terminus, King's Bridge, 1854

Ulster railway terminus, Belfast

The elegance and comfort of first and second-class carriages running on a smooth, standardised permanent way represented a whole new concept of travel far removed from the cramped stage coaches and open cars of a decade earlier. On a humbler level, third-class travel and workingmen's trains were to provide a service for people who, in the past, had more often than not to go on foot if they were to travel at all. Before the railways, of course, there had been people who travelled for pleasure urged on by curiosity. But such journeys were difficult, often uncomfortable and only for the few. The railways made travel for pleasure easy, and the imposing new railway hotels, as at Galway and Killarney, and the station refreshment rooms were to make travel still more agreeable in the course of the 1850s. The tourist ticket and the excursion were further inducements to see the country. This new kind of popular travel, as we now know, was to become an accepted factor in daily life.

The railways made an impact on the Irish scene in another way. They came into existence with the trappings of solidarity, if only to quieten the fears of timid passengers, or investors, presented with the strange locomotives for the first time. The railway companies built not only hotels but impressive terminal buildings such as Kingsbridge and the Broadstone in Dublin. The former was described by a traveller in 1852, as a 'fine building . . . two stories high with wings the height of the basement story, from which rise graceful clock towers; the whole faced with mountain granite; contributing one of the noblest of the modern architectural ornaments of Dublin . . . The interior of the station nearly equals anything of the kind in England.' The local stations, often very distinctive in architecture, projected the same image of security and confidence in the country towns. The railways were new but they were safe and represented a high standard of speed and comfort.

The railways also helped to integrate the economy and to strengthen urban influences in commercial and cultural terms. Indeed, along with emigration and the national schools, the railways might well be seen as yet another factor which contributed to the weakening of those social and economic conditions which had helped to preserve old traditions and cultural patterns in Irish rural society.

8 The Golden Age of Irish Railways

Joseph Lee

THE 'GOLDEN AGE' may sound rather a question-begging description of Irish railway history between the Famine and the First World War. Was it really a period of peak prosperity for all the interests involved: shareholders, managers, workers and customers? Or did some fare better than others?

On the eve of the First World War there were approximately 50,000 shareholders, most of whom were Irish, holding the £45,000,000 of Irish railway stock and earning an average dividend of almost four per cent. Although this hardly sounds a golden return, it compared favourably with the two and a half to three per cent yield on government funds, the main alternative for security-seeking rentier investors. Indeed, only four out of fourteen European railway systems recorded a higher return on capital. Four per cent also compared quite well with average English railway dividends, and certainly acquired a retrospective glow from the viewpoint of the dismal returns of the inter-war years. It is worth noting that the better dividends of five per cent or higher were paid to a large number of relatively small investors: the 5,000 ordinary shareholders in the Great Northern held, on average £750 stock, the 7,500 in the Great Southern and Western, £700. 'Small investor' is itself, of course, a relative term implying an annual dividend of about £40, the equivalent of an unskilled labourer's total annual income.

It may seem surprising in view of the much denser traffic on British lines, that Irish dividends could compare with English, but traffic receipts constitute only one of three key variables influencing dividends, the other two being working expenses and construction costs. Working expenses were about the same in Ireland as in England, hovering around sixty per cent of gross receipts.

William Dargan

III

The total amount of capital on which dividends had to be paid was much smaller in Ireland, because construction costs per mile were nearly three times cheaper than in Britain. To keep the comparisons within the country, the Dublin and Kingstown, the most prosperous Irish company, generally paid eight per cent. Had it been built at the Irish average of £15,000 per mile, instead of costing £60,000, its shareholders would have received a handsome thirty-two per cent. Cheap labour was the most important factor in keeping construction costs low, but tribute should also be paid to the efficiency of the great contractor, William Dargan, and of the outstanding engineer, Sir John McNeill.

It was, of course, extremely fortunate for the shareholders that traffic was only one factor affecting dividends, because traffic was very light indeed. Receipts for the country as a whole fluctuated fairly narrowly around the £1,000 per mile mark, though this steadiness in gross income conceals considerable changes in the composition of traffic. Passenger travel was progressively democratised, catering increasingly for the people of small property—the third class. Between 1860 and 1910, the number of first and second-class-passengers fell from five to three million, but the number of third-class bounded up from five to twenty-five million. The number of journeys per annum per head of adult population rose from three in 1860 to thirteen in 1910: in other words the increase in the propensity to travel within the country more than sufficed to maintain the density of passenger traffic in the face of rapidly falling population and the extension of track westwards into the poorer parts of the country. Passenger traffic always remained more important than goods, accounting for about fifty-five per cent of total receipts.

Apart from population decline, most of the other major problems confronting railway managers also lay outside their control. Consider for instance, the seasonal nature of traffic. Passenger receipts in 1910 averaged only £30,000 a week in winter, compared with £50,000 in summer, and at peak excursion and holiday week-end periods like Easter and Whistun, traffic could increase five fold on seaside lines to Bray, Bangor, Tramore and Passage West. However gratifyingly this reflected growing leisure among the poorer classes, it created enormous headaches for the railway managers and workers. Seasonality was also a major problem in the goods sector. Butter exports, for example, lasted only from May to November, being virtually non-existent during the remaining months. This seasonal nature of traffic naturally involved extremely wasteful use of rolling stock.

Apart from the problems created by seasonal traffic, the whole economic and geographic structure of the country was unfavourable from the railwayman's viewpoint. Because the main production and consumption centres were on the east coast, much of the foreign trade of the country never came near the railways. The largest single export, linen, accounting for one-fifth of total exports, was dispatched directly from Belfast. There was little mineral traffic, so lucrative on English lines, as four-fifths of all coal imports were consumed immediately in the ports, never finding their way on to the railway system. It must be admitted that the methods used for forecasting traffic were so crude that most promoters had only the vaguest idea of the probable size of their market. Traffic takers were normally posted along the route for a fortnight, and their results doubled or trebled to allow for the increase in traffic invariably anticipated from improved communications. Traffic takers sometimes counted everything that moved above ground as potential railway traffic: funerals, hunts, farmers coming a mile or two to the nearest market were all considered potential railway clients. The traffic takers guessed the average distance to be travelled by each passenger or animal, and the average fare to be charged. The Dublin and Drogheda assumed an average fare of four shillings in forecasting its revenue: in practice this worked out at two shillings, immediately slashing all calculations by half. The Belfast and Ballymena, serving the district least affected by famine, was still fifty per cent short of its expected traffic five years after opening.

The railway manager had, it is true, some compensations for these headaches. He faced little competition from other forms of transport, and not much from other railways except in certain areas. Rate wars did occasionally flare up between the various lines, but they were a far cry from the problems subsequently posed by the motor car, the bus and the lorry.

If the companies served their shareholders reasonably satisfactorily, was

Locomotive built at Inchicore in 1875

The railway was designed to bring freight to the quayside at Queenstown, (Cobh) 1900

this, as a Committee of Enquiry in 1922 asserted, at the expense of their workers? In 1913 the railways paid £1·5 million in wages and salaries, which accounted for over fifty per cent of the total working expenses, quite a high proportion by European standards. Railway wages compared very favourably with wages in other sectors and, by the admittedly undemanding standards of the times, the railways must be reckoned good employers. By levelling up most rural wages to the Dublin and Belfast levels, a move certainly not dictated by any shortage of local labour, they paid well above the market rate in many areas, and the fringe benefit of a uniform added to the attractions of a railway life.

A clerk's position in particular was quite comfortable, as the huge number of applications, often over a hundred for ordinary clerkships, testifies. The average outdoor wage in 1912 was about £1 a week, the average indoor salary £3. The working day for outdoor labour was reduced from thirteen hours in 1850 to eleven in 1913, but the clerk had a comfortable eight hour day from the beginning. Promotion prospects, particularly in the early years of rapidly expanding mileage, were exceptionally promising. The Assistant Secretary of the Great Southern and Western, enjoying an annual salary of

114

£350 in 1856, had entered as a junior clerk on only £40 ten years before. Handsome golden handshakes sweetened the sorrow of parting even for failed managers and senior officials, who frequently received up to two years' salary to give them ample time to find situations more congenial to their lack of talents.

Outdoor workers had a much harder time of it. Nevertheless resignations, especially among the unskilled, were few indeed, because of the dearth of alternative employment. Though the long hours may suggest grinding exploitation, it would be wrong to infer that railway life rivalled the reign of terror associated with the initial stages of industrialisation in factory and mines. The light traffic—no more than ten trains a day at most stations—required only intermittent exertion. The drowsy, loitering, conversational atmosphere of a country station—and even of many urban ones—infrequently punctuated by unwonted bustle on the arrival of a train, bore little relation to the machine-dominated drudgery of the factory. The station masters at Thurles and Templemore were taking advantage of these lethargic, un-exacting conditions, where one might hope not to be missed, when they were unfortunate enough to be caught and reprimanded 'for leaving their station without permission . . . and proceeding per train to the Cashel Races without paying their fares . . . and afterwards making false statements as to the cause of their absence'. The Dublin and Drogheda had to forbid its pointsmen to keep dogs, to prevent them putting their unoccupied time to profitable use by poaching on Lord Gormanston's estates. A station master's weakness for milk led to the sad case of Clotworthy's cow, when, in the intonations of the Ulster's minute book 'a cow belonging to the manager of the Portadown station had been put to graze on the company's ground, and had strayed on the line, and was killed', whereon Clotworthy inadvisedly claimed compensation, and the directors, taking an extremely dim view of the matter, decided to 'express to Mr Clotworthy, through the Chairman, their high displeasure at his putting his cow on the company's ground at all'. The board of the Dundalk and Enniskillen, meeting in Dublin, could hardly show similar high displeasure by censuring the staff at Dundalk, fifty miles away, whose collective spontaneous decision to take a day off, for the worthy motive of attending a local director's funeral, resulted in a horde of claims from irate passengers wrongfully detained and misdirected by the casual replacements roped in for the day by the regular staff. As Portadown and Dundalk were two of the busiest stations in the country, the cow and the funeral reflect the relaxed rhythm of Irish railway life.

The directors were paternalistic, priding themselves on a sense of conscious rectitude towards their workers. They were reluctant to dismiss employees for ill-health, doing their best to find less strenuous employment within the company for them, and they went out of their way to get jobs for the orphans of their workers. Dismissals ran at a rate of about five per cent per annum. Being mainly for drunkenness, they were virtually confined to the outdoor staff, an extremely unfair consequence of their longer working hours, for they had to get drunk on company time if they were to get properly drunk at all, whereas clerical staff, with much shorter working hours, could imbibe behind discreetly drawn suburban curtains. Dismissals were considered on their individual merits, however, and the worst that can be said about the directors is that they were arbitrary, not that they were vindictive. There was certainly no draconian code.

The most common charge of all levelled at the companies was not that they served their shareholders at the expense of their workers, but at the expense of the public. It was widely felt that rates were set at a level to earn the highest dividends for the investors rather than at a level that would best develop the country's resources. Numerous enquiries were held into railway services, the same complaints being reiterated generation after generation. However golden it may have been in other respects this certainly was not an age of golden opinions about the railways. Unfortunately, there can scarcely be a topic of economic interest about which even well-informed public opinion revealed such confused and muddled thinking as railway charges. The bulk of the evidence of the 267 witnesses examined by the last great pre-war enquiry, during 1906–9, bears massive testimony to the immense ignorance of the public. Most of the hostile witnesses collapsed under cross-examination and, had all their recommendations been followed, no fewer than another eighty-three railway lines would have been built in an already densely railwayised country. Even more extraordinary than the witnesses' evidence is the majority report which contains some of the most startling non-sequiturs in the whole history of Irish economic comment. The commissioners of enquiry shared at the outset the general conviction that exorbitant rates were strangling the trade of the country and that public ownership offered the only solution. When the evidence failed to confirm these *a priori* assumptions about the pernicious effects of transport costs, they resorted to a series of sweeping and unsupported comparisons of the situation in other countries, concluding with the assertion that a success of state railways in Australia constituted a powerful argument in favour of state railways at home, as if a more irrelevant comparison with Ireland could be found on the face of the globe than Australia.

Their reflections on the acquisition of Irish lines by English companies provided useful arguments for Ulster unionists. The main instance had been the takeover of the Belfast and Northern Counties railway by the English Midland in 1905. Belfast witnesses so unanimously approved of this step that the report conceded that 'the introduction of English capital into Irish railway companies has been a distinct material advantage to the poorer country,' but nevertheless advised against any further attempt to attract English capital because of the hostility of nationalist public opinion, which should carry greater weight than the intrinsic merits of the case.

All informed opinion, it is true, did share the commissioners' belief that Ireland had too many railway companies—sixteen effective ones, in fact. Sixteen companies were undoubtedly far too many, but in practice, three concerns, the Great Southern and Western, the Great Northern and the Midland Great Western controlled three-quarters of the traffic, and it was by no means clear that the merging of these three would improve the system because, in effect, they served different economies. The north, the south and the west of Ireland were three distinct economic areas, both for passenger and goods traffic, each having far more in common with its English market than with the other two areas. In July 1907, for instance, at the height of the tourist season, only two passengers a day were booked through the Great Northern for the Great Southern and Western. Railway directorates were

Rail viaduct, Ballydehob, Co. Cork, in the 1880s

GSR engine, 1913

already so interlocked that little internal secrecy survived between companies, and even the most committed supporters of unification dared not claim that it would save more than £50,000 per annum in administrative rationalisation, a saving of less than three per cent on total working costs. There was, in short, no panacea solution to the problem of railway rates, and it is ironic that after so many people had advocated state management on the grounds that it would lead to a reduction in rates, the first action of the state when it assumed control of the system in the First World War was not to lower, but to raise charges, though admittedly by then circumstances had changed greatly from those envisaged by advocates of state control.

While there is no *a priori* reason why what was good for the railways should be good for Ireland, little weight can be attached to the belief that Irish trade was strangled by railway rates. It would be surprising if directorates which included some of the shrewdest businessmen in the country—William Martin Murphy, Sir William Goulding, Frederick Pim, John Jameson, William Cairnes—would have attempted to hinder development which might benefit their own firms. Many of the critics were groping towards the concept of marginal social, as distinct from marginal private benefit: that while low

118

railway rates might harm the shareholders they would benefit the country by encouraging industrial and agricultural development. This would have been a powerful argument if the critics could have shown how lower rates would have encouraged extensive economic growth. But there are indications that the railways themselves, in their empirical fashion, may have found the solution to this problem. Cheap import rates possibly prevented local manufacturers from expanding in a few instances, but the bulk of complaints on this score must be dismissed because transport costs formed such a small proportion of total selling costs. It is significant that the offer of the Department of Agriculture and Technical Instruction to subsidise the transport costs of traders in the congested districts who could show that a reduction in existing railway rates would enable their business to develop, elicited not a solitary application. It can be categorically claimed that the miserable performance of Irish agricultural exports in the British market after 1880 cannot be blamed on poor railway services. It was generally conceded, even by William Field, a nationalist M.P. and the most articulate representative of the interests of the cattle trade, that Irish railway services improved most rapidly at precisely the period when the Irish share of the British market declined most seriously.

It can be seen therefore that the description 'golden age' applies to railway life as seen mainly through the eyes of shareholders, managers and clerks. But it is also true that the interests of these groups were not as opposed to those of workers and travellers as has sometimes been alleged. If the term 'golden age' is an exaggeration, it is an exaggeration in the right direction.

9 Sea Communications in the Nineteenth Century

Oliver MacDonagh

THE NINETEENTH century has been accredited with so many revolutions that one hesitates to add another to its battle honours. But whether we call it revolution or not—and I think one should—the nineteenth century certainly saw an amazing transformation in almost every aspect of sea-traffic. I draw attention to this transformation at the outset because these changes in the world at large were the main determinants of Ireland's maritime history between the Act of Union and the First World War; and for an explanation of the relative decline of Irish shipping in these years, we must look, essentially, to the increase and development of international sea communications overall.

Several interlocking factors contributed to the general transformation. One set consisted of technological advances. To begin with, the period 1815 to 1875 was the golden age of sailing-ship design. In sum, the improvements of these sixty years probably exceeded those of the preceding six hundred. The intense naval warfare of the revolutionary and Napoleonic era acted as a forcing house for ship design in much the same way as the Second World War served aviation in our own day. After 1815 the lessons learned in the hard school of war were quickly transferred to the merchant vessel. Other post-war pressures, mainly commercial, ensured that this new drive for ever greater speed, size and manoeuvrability was maintained. It reached its climax in the generation of magnificent tea-clippers, epitomised in the popular imagination by the *Cutty Sark*. The second major change in ship construction, which also of course contributed to the first, was the replacement of wood by iron, and later the partial replacement of iron by steel. Originally employed to overcome the size-limitation imposed by wooden hulls, iron came gradually to predominate as the building material even for sailing ships during the middle decades of the nineteenth century. Iron—and still more so steel—rendered vessels stronger, lighter, larger and cheaper to build and maintain. The third great technological change—or rather changes—were the substitution of steam power for sail, and later the substitution of the screw propeller for the paddle wheel. Needless to say, steam and the screw propeller furthered the causes of speed, spaciousness and manoeuvrability in vessels, but they also served a new end; predictability. Steam made it possible to lay out and adhere to fixed schedules of sailings and fixed departure and arrival times, in a way which sail, always to some degree dependent on the weather, could never do. Steam power in shipping advanced in stages. As early as the 1820s it had established itself for much of the estuary and cross-channel work, such as the navigation of Cork Harbour or the passage of the Irish Sea. In the 1840s it established itself in the highest levels of the transatlantic trade, for the carriage of mails, of wealthy passengers and of cargo of great

The 'Great Eastern' leaving Sheerness with the Atlantic telegraph cable on board, 1866

Stranraer mail boat at Larne, late nineteenth century.

value and small bulk. By the end of the American Civil War in 1865 it had captured almost the entire North American passenger business, and most of that to Australasia, India and the Far East. By 1900 it had come to dominate even cargo shipping, although a few pockets, such as the guano trade where speed counted for little and cheapness for much, remained the preserve of sail, and one or two schooner centres such as Arklow managed to survive down to 1914.

Part cause and part effect of this technological revolution was the vast expansion and regularisation of international trade in the nineteenth century. An indication of the pace and scale of the upsurge is the growth of the British merchant marine by 400 to 500 per cent between 1800 and 1900. Meanwhile year by year the channel, the Atlantic and even more remote sea-routes were being criss-crossed by ever more elaborate and dependable patterns of shipping. All this meant the growing domination of the large iron vessel and of a few great international ports. This is not to say that the smaller ocean-going vessel of, say, 100 to 300 tons had disappeared completely by 1900, or that the smaller port with, say, 100 to 300 arrivals and departures annually had ceased to operate. But whereas the small vessel and the small port had been the staple of sea-communications in 1800, by 1850 both were clearly in decline and after 1900 their role was secondary and minor. The change was roughly equivalent to that whereby the factory and the large-scale manufacturer superseded the handloom and the craftsman weaver.

In describing the general change which sea-communications underwent between the American Revolution and the First World War, I have already indicated, indirectly, much of the fate of Irish shipping in the same years. Even after a marked increase in Irish maritime activity in the closing decades of the eighteenth century, by 1800 the Irish shipping industry was still very small in scale, and much divided in ownership and port of origin. The total Irish-registered tonnage of vessels of 100 tons and over was less than 50,000. No port had a sizeable merchant fleet, even by contemporary standards. That of the leading Irish port of the day, Dublin, was under 20,000 tons in all. The fleet of its nearest rival, Cork, was only half this size, while the next four ports in order of importance, Belfast, Waterford, Newry and Derry, possessed a mere 3–5,000 registered tons each. The vessels themselves were minuscule. Very few Irish ships exceeded 200 tons in size; in fact, few were as large as 150. As all this suggests, much of Ireland's share of the world's carrying trade was carried already in British holds. To revive our metaphor, Ireland's maritime situation at the opening of the nineteenth century was that of the petty workshop and hand-worker on the eve of the Industrial Revolution.

Given the minute scale and the undeveloped nature of the industry, the decline in Irish shipping was almost inevitable in the circumstances of the nineteenth century. But its plight was worsened by Ireland's geographical proximity to and political connection with Great Britain. True, the Union brought some gains initially. Irish shipping, placed on an equal footing with British, now enjoyed the protection and other advantages of the Navigation Acts. This enabled Irish vessels to take a modest share of the rapidly-growing corn importation trade, and perhaps also to advance a little, for a time, in the great triangular traffic between the United Kingdom, the West Indies and North America. But the gains were counter-balanced by adverse factors, and these soon prevailed. The essential adverse factor was that Great Britain was the leading maritime power of the century, with universal sea interests, the world's largest merchant marine, boundless capital for investment and the lion's share of the international carrying trade; and three of her greatest ports, Liverpool, Glasgow and Bristol, lay within a hundred miles of the Irish coast. There could be no question of protecting Irish shipping from British competition under the Act of Union—not indeed that this would have been practicable before the statute. Half way through our period, the repeal of the Navigation Acts in 1849 removed the only significant advantage which Irish shipping had enjoyed over British and foreign competition, particularly the world's second sea-power, the United States, in both the Atlantic and the European seas. In the mid-century, therefore, Ireland was open, to a greater degree perhaps than any comparable nation, to the mounting blast of the revolution in sea-communications, which was to give the spoils to the large and powerful, and send the small and puny to the wall.

The result was substantially what might have been predicted. Before the 1860s when there was still a place on the ocean for the small, slow, wooden vessel, and still a place for the small port as an export centre, the Irish shipping industry managed to continue more or less upon its accustomed scale. In fact in some respects it showed remarkable promise. With the growing demand in Great Britain for Irish agricultural produce, and in particular for cattle, and with a vast increase in passenger traffic between the two islands, the tonnage of Irish-registered vessels engaged in the cross-channel trade doubled between 1800 and 1850. There were dreams of a great Irish entrepôt for the Atlantic traffic. Even the sober Sir Robert Kane argued in his celebrated *Industrial Resources of Ireland* in 1843:

IT IS SOMETIMES supposed that the introduction of steam upon the Atlantic has neutralised the westerly position of this country and removed the disadvantages of the English channel navigation. This is not the case. The freight of goods in steam vessels on long voyages is far too high to allow of their being generally used . . . and passengers also would naturally prefer to start from the extremest point of land. Railroads from Dublin to Valentia, Berehaven or Tarbert, [Kane concluded] would render Ireland the leading highway between the hemispheres.

There were moments when it seemed that some such vision might be realised. The first steam crossing of the Atlantic, from Cork to New York in 1838, was made by a vessel of the St George Steam Packet Company of Cork, the *Sirius,* 260 tons. It was hoped, vainly as things turned out, that the voyage of the *Sirius* would inaugurate a major transatlantic line. Twenty years later, upon the completion of the railway link between Dublin and Galway, an attempt was made to establish Galway as the eastern terminus for Atlantic mails. John Lever of Manchester set up the Atlantic Royal Mail Steam Navigation Company, generally known as the Galway line, with three chartered steamships; and in January 1859 he won a twelve-month mail contract for a Galway–St John, Newfoundland run in seven days. Again, in the first half of the nineteenth century, at no less than three centres in Ireland—Waterford, Cork and Derry—shipbuilding promised at one stage or other to flower into a major industry. Cork's pioneering work seemed particularly hopeful. As early as 1815 a paddle steamer, *The City of Cork,* was built at Passage West. As early as 1845 an iron-hulled vessel was built at Cork itself, and in the following year a screw-propeller steamer, the *Blarney*, was launched for the Cork Steamship Company.

All this, however, represented little more than a postponement of the inevitable. 1849, the year in which the Navigation Acts were repealed, also marked the zenith of the development of Irish shipping under the Act of Union. Thereafter the Irish share of even the cross-channel traffic with Great Britain began to fall; and the railway companies, amongst other British lines, were to be increasingly active competitors on the Irish Sea in the closing decades of the nineteenth century. The City of Dublin Steam Packet Company which had fought a brisk battle with the Post Office and Admiralty steamers on the Dublin–Liverpool route between 1826 and 1839, did secure the main London mail contract in 1850, and held it against all opposition down to the First World War. But such successes were few. Overall, Irish vessels lost ground steadily in the cross-channel trade after 1850. It was, however, the Irish ocean-going traffic which fell away most dramatically. Here the

The 'Sirius', 1847

GLASGOW, DUBLIN

AND

Londonderry Steam Packet Company's

(LAIRD LINE)

TOURS

FROM GLASGOW TO THE WEST OF IRELAND,

FOR

CONNEMARA, KILKEE, LIMERICK,

KILLALOE and KILLARNEY.

TOUR No. 11.

To Sligo by Steamer; Rail thence to Kilkee. *via* Ennis; Passengers may break journey at Sligo for Lough Gill Claremorris for Achill; Athenry for Galway and Connemara; Ennistymon for Famous Spa and Baths; Lahinch for Cliffs of Moher. Return by same route.

FARES :—Cabin and 1st Class, 37/-; Cabin and 2nd Class, 33/-;
Steerage and 3rd Class, 18/-.

TOUR No. 12.

To Sligo by Steamer; Rail thence to Killaloe. Passengers may break journey at Sligo for Lough Gill; Claremorris for Achill; Athenry for Galway and Connemara; Ennis for Kilkee, etc.; Limerick for the River Shannon, Adare and Quin Abbey Ruins. Return by same route.

FARES :—Cabin and 1st Class, 35/-; Cabin and 2nd Class, 30/-;
Steerage and 3rd Class, 16/-.

TOUR No. 13.

To Sligo by Steamer; Rail thence to Tralee for Killarney. Passengers may break journey at Sligo for Lough Gill; Claremorris for Achill; Athenry for Galway and Connemara; Ennis for Kilkee; Limerick for River Shannon; Listowel for Ballybunion, reached by novel Lartigue Railway. Return by same route.

FARES :—Cabin and 1st Class, 35/-; Cabin and 2nd Class, 30/-;
Steerage and 3rd Class, 16/-.

These Tickets are available for Return up to 31st Dec., 1898.

decline was quite marked in the 1850s; but this was merely the prelude to an all but total collapse in the succeeding decade. By 1870 Irish vessels had been virtually swept from the Atlantic, the only ocean in which they had plied to any significant extent. Even in the 1830s and 1840s, Irish overseas exports, especially of more perishable goods such as pork, stout or butter, had been sent increasingly to the major British ports, and in particular to Liverpool, for trans-shipment. The early decline of Dublin as the export centre for Belfast linens was another straw which showed how the wind was blowing. But it was in the 1850s that the power of the vast port and of the large-scale shipper became altogether irresistible.

Correspondingly Galway was never to become a European terminus; Lever's venture failed miserably within three years. True, it was several decades before the citizens of Galway relinquished the dream of their city as the gateway to the continent of Europe. As T. P. O'Connor, their member of parliament from 1880 to 1885, later observed: 'the vision of Galway as a shipping centre could not be laid.' But vision it remained. At Cork, Waterford and Derry, shipbuilding continued in the third quarter of the nineteenth century, but only on its initial petty scale. By the fourth quarter, the industry was almost dead in each of these three centres.

Ironically enough the collapse of the Irish ocean-going traffic coincided more or less with the growth of a major shipbuilding industry in Belfast in the late 1850s and the 1860s; and this was soon to be followed by the development of a major passenger port at Cobh, and of a major naval base and dockyard in Cork Harbour. But these last were really manifestations of the new scale, complexity and internationalisation of sea-communications. None of the giant vessels launched at Belfast by Harland and Wolff or Workman, Clarke and Company between 1860 and 1914 was to be registered at an Irish port. The liners which called at Cobh were based, not at Galway, Limerick or Dublin, but at New York, Le Havre, Liverpool or Hamburg. The extension to the naval base, and the erection of a graving dock at Haulbowline, were mere items in the world-extended chain of British naval power. Not until the Second World War was there to be, in Mr Basil Peterson's phrase, 'a turn of the tide'. It was only in 1941, and as a consequence of the great national emergency, that the first steps were taken towards the re-creation of the Irish shipping industry.

Let us now try to translate this story into more human and specific terms.

The opening of the new channel at Belfast harbour, 1849

Perhaps the best index of the decline of Irish shipping in the nineteenth century lies in the history of Ireland's saddest export, people. At first, when Irish emigration to North America re-commenced after the Napoleonic Wars, the great bulk of the emigrants sailed, as they had done in the eighteenth century, upon small Irish vessels from small Irish ports. Down to 1825 they numbered on average some 20,000 per annum, and the carriage of such a body was well within the resources of the Irish transatlantic vessels. But when in the early 1830s, the average annual emigration rose to over 60,000, Liverpool, now readily accessible by steam packet, became almost overnight the main embarkation centre for Irish emigrants. In fact during the years 1830–46 well over half the Irish emigrants for North America embarked there, and in the decade 1846–56 when Irish emigration averaged nearly 200,000 persons per annum, the proportion embarking at Liverpool increased to four in five. By the end of the American Civil War, the traditional Irish passenger trade in vessels of 200–50 tons had been practically extinguished.

The rise of Liverpool was all the more remarkable because that port had several grievous disadvantages for Irish emigrants. To embark there exposed the emigrants to the additional discomforts, dangers and expense—none of

128

them small matters before 1850—of a preliminary steamer crossing. Secondly, the very factor which gave Liverpool its eminence, the vast extent of its maritime activity, rendered it thoroughly unsuitable for emigrants. Dock regulations forbade the use of fires or lights on vessels, and cargo was often stowed up to the last minute. Consequently no passenger was permitted to go aboard his vessel until it was almost time to sail, and vessels commonly cast off in the midst of wild confusion. Moreover Liverpool was growing rapidly, and the spread of foul slums along its docklands laid it open to every infection. This was important for the Irish because, as a result of the prohibition upon early embarkation, almost all of them had to spend two or three nights in lodgings before they sailed. The charges for lodgings were low, but the places themselves were seedbeds of disease and fraud. People lay packed together on straw or cellar floors, with neither fire nor light, and the lodging keepers made their profits from the sale of whiskey, and commissions from the ship-chandlers to whom they sent their unwary guests. Such living conditions and such practices were poor preparation for the voyage; and there is no doubt that many of the epidemics which ravaged emigrants at sea had their origin in these surroundings.

How did Liverpool come to capture an essentially Irish business in such circumstances? The answer lies in the nature of transatlantic shipping in the years 1800–60. For the run-of-the-mill cargo ships on the North Atlantic, emigrants were a subsidiary interest, but an indispensable subsidiary. They were accepted by most owners and captains (who often had no direct responsibility for the passage contract) only with the utmost reluctance; but

Entrance to Cork Harbour, Queenstown in the distance, Spike Island in the middle distance, 1854

EXCURSIONS TO LIVERPOOL

Via Waterford and direct Steamer

CHEAP TICKETS will be issued from the undermentioned Stations to LIVERPOOL, via Waterford and thence by the Waterford Steamship Co.'s

Splendidly appointed Passenger Steamers.

TICKETS AVAILABLE FOR RETURN FOR ONE CALENDAR MONTH

On Wednesdays, 1st, 8th, 15th, 22nd, 29th June; 6th, 13th, 20th 27th July; 3rd, 10th, 17th, 24th & 31st August; 7th, 14th, 21st, 28th September, 189.

	RETURN FARES. 1st Class	3rd Class		RETURN FARES. 1st Class	3rd Class
SWINFORD CLAREMORRIS TUAM ATHENRY	30/-	15,-	NEWCASTLE RATHKEALE FOYNES	25/-	15/-
ENNIS LIMERICK	25/-	15,-	LIMERICK JCT. TIPPERARY CAHIR THURLES FETHARD	25,-	12/6
TRALEE LISTOWEL ABBEYFEALE	30,-	15,-			

As the Cabin Accommodation is limited to a certain number of Passengers application for First Class Tickets should be made at the respective Stations not later than three days in advance of above dates.

Children under 3 years of age, Free; above 3 and under 12 years, Half Fares.

Passengers will require to leave Limerick by the 8.20 a.m. Train to be in time for Steamer when sailing before 4.0 p.m. Branch Line Stations not having connections with this Train can book Passengers by the last Train on the dates preceding the Excursions. When Steamer sails at 4.0 p.m. or later, Passengers can be booked by connecting trains due in Waterford 3.27 p.m.

The Waterford Steamship Company's Berth is at Trafalgar Dock, Liverpool.

THROUGH TICKETS.—Through Tickets, permitting the Holders thereof to travel to and from the places off the Company's line, are issued solely for the convenience of the holders, and the acceptance thereof is to be taken as conclusive evidence of an agreement that the respective Companies on whose Railways, Coaches, or Steamboats, such tickets are available are not under any circumstances to incur any responsibility for or in respect of any delay or detention of, or injury or damage to either the person or the property of the holder; or for or in respect of any loss of life or property of any holder caused or arising off their respective lines; nor for or in respect of the non-arrival of their respective Trains, Coaches, or Steamboats, in time for the nominally corresponding Trains, Coaches, or Steamboats, of any or either of the other Companies, or of any other Company or person whatsoever; nor for the failure of such other Companies or persons, or any or either of them, to run any nominally corresponding Trains, Coaches, or Steamboats.

The contract and liability of each Company are in each case limited exclusively to its own lines of Railway, Coaches, and Steamboats. Any money received by this Company for Carriage off its own line of Railway, Coaches, or Steamboats, will be so received for the sole purpose of being paid over to the other Companies or persons on whose lines of Railway, Coaches, or Steamboats, the Through Tickets for which such money is paid are available. Through Tickets (where the journey is not continuous) do not include the cost of transfer or conveyance between any termini of the respective Companies, or between any Stations, Coaches, and Steamboats, or any or either of them, of any or either of such Companies or persons respectively, and the Companies do not undertake such transfer or conveyance, or any responsibility in connection therewith.

they were a necessary evil. Occasionally shipping was scarce enough and freights high enough for shippers to escape the irritations and restrictions which carrying passengers involved. But in general passengers were unavoidable. 'Unless they transport emigrants,' wrote Wilmot Horton in 1825, 'the Irish Timber Vessels necessarily go without freight.' The Irish Atlantic ships were principally engaged in the timber, potash and grain trades, and predominantly in the first. The Liverpool vessels depended mainly upon cotton and timber. Now all these imports demanded ships with large broad holds, for which there were either no outward cargoes at all or insufficient outward cargoes to fill the space. In consequence the shippers were forced to turn to emigrants. None wanted them as such; but the alternative was to sail in ballast and at a total loss.

Although the volume of emigration fluctuated from year to year, by the mid-1820s, it was sufficiently regular to constitute a part of most transatlantic traffic patterns. Thus, for example, all Limerick's ocean-going vessels, which were primarily engaged in the import of timber, staves and deal, carried passengers to Quebec or St John (or to Boston or New York before proceeding northwards) during the spring and summer. The Limerick ships then spent the winter months in the coastal trade in provisions and coal with Glasgow, Liverpool or South Wales. Derry had a similar pattern of trade with Philadelphia, whence she had imported flour and maize for decades, for the most part sending only emigrants in return. Many of the Liverpool vessels followed a triangular course; from New York to New Orleans, Mobile or Charleston with manufactured goods, coal or hard cargoes; from the southern American port to Liverpool with cotton; and from Liverpool back to New York with emigrants, and perhaps a little chemicals or pig or bar iron.

You may have noticed earlier that although the proportion of Irish emigration emanating from Irish ports fell steadily between 1825 and 1855, the actual volume remained more or less constant, at something between 25,000 and 35,000 persons per annum. In great emergencies such as the outrush of 1847, when any vessel drawing eighty tons which floated might be pressed into service, the number leaving Ireland directly was larger. But generally speaking, 35,000 passengers was the Irish ceiling, and at that the embarkations were well distributed amongst the Irish ports. During the twenty years of heaviest emigration, 1840–60, both Cork and Limerick averaged some 7,000 emigrants annually; Sligo, Derry, Belfast, New Ross and Waterford averaged

131

Liner built by Harland & Wolff in 1874 for the White Star line

about half this number each; and several other Irish ports sent out their few hundreds regularly. The balance, however large or small, had to leave through Liverpool. Irish newspapers and Irish shippers might deplore the loss of trade, but the fact was that emigration was forced to follow the established lanes of transatlantic commerce, and Ireland had neither the shipping nor the imports to capture the new movement. Liverpool alone could provide the vessels in sufficient numbers. Liverpool alone could build up packet lines in half a decade, and cope with the immense business in remittance and prepaid passages which followed in the wake of Irish and (to a lesser extent) of German and British mass emigration.

Thus the history of emigration in the nineteenth century brings out very clearly the limited nature of contemporary Irish shipping. The Irish passenger trade could never expand significantly, because passengers were a secondary consideration for the shippers, and because the scale of their operations was very small. The story of the loss of even this modest business is equally illuminating. After 1850 the mass carriage of emigrants from Europe became an important trade in its own right. Much larger vessels, specifically designed for several hundred passengers, were now being built. Steam was no longer the privilege of the upper ten thousand of Atlantic voyagers. Standards of comfort and safety rose steadily, partly through new legislative requirements, partly through a change in the level of expectation. Yet so great were the economies of scale and concentration that by the mid-1850s Liverpool vessels, whose fares had hitherto been considerably more expensive than the

Irish, began to add a price advantage to the rest. The Irish-Atlantic trade, already suffering from the increasing cheapness and ease of routing Irish imports and exports through the major British ports, was now hit upon its second wing, once the overwhelming superiority of Liverpool as the departure point for Irish emigrants became established.

In describing the fate of Irish shipping in the nineteenth century, I have necessarily had to dwell in gloom. Until the middle decades of the present century, when the combination of political independence and a realistic assessment of the nature of modern sea-communications enabled this industry to be re-founded upon a new basis, Ireland was at the mercy, more or less, of irresistible international trends. But few historical phenomena can be accounted wholly as loss or wholly as gain. There was of course another side to the picture which I have painted. Who would wish that the miseries and dangers, the long uncertain passages and the disease and hunger which so often accompanied the early Irish passenger trade should have been perpetuated? Who would wish that the onset of steam power, iron vessels, low fares and cheap freights should have been postponed, although their advance implied the rise of Liverpool and Glasgow? As always it would have been inhumane, as well as futile, to work against the grain of technological improvement and economic growth. The thing was—and is—to understand them and to plan accordingly.

10 The Return to the Roads

Miriam Daly

AN ADVERTISEMENT in the *Irish Motor Annual* for 1911 described the motor car as 'the last expression of combined engineering skill and beautiful workmanship'. In the same issue a contributor asserted: 'By the side of the road vehicle today the railway is already largely a back number' and went on ambiguously, 'By the same standard of comparison the horse is dead'[1]. By this date motoring had emerged from its pioneering phase when the emphasis had been on experiment, innovation and speed and motorists were either enthusiasts or upper-class converts to the new pastime. It was already firmly established as an acceptable, convenient form of private or public transport for passengers or goods. The impact of this competition was not reflected in the receipts of the railway companies however until they were handed back by the government to the companies in August 1921.[2]

During the pioneering phase, motoring developed quickly in Ireland. In 1898 the Motor Car Club, which represented motoring interests throughout the British Isles, was replaced by the more formal Royal Automobile Club of Great Britain and Ireland. By 1901 Irish motorists were sufficiently numerous and confident to organise the Irish Automobile Club and promote the first Irish rally, 'The Great Motor Tour' as it was called, an enjoyable journey of 1,000 miles. R. J. Macredy, who organised the procession of ten cars which took a fortnight over the journey, had been a noted cyclist, founder of *The Irish Cyclist* and editor of *Motor News*. He was the moving spirit behind the introduction of the Automobile Association (founded 1905) to Ireland as a motorists' protection organisation to defend motorists who were prosecuted for exceeding the 20 m.p.h. speed limit, and as a pressure group to secure the road improvements which the convenience of motorists and cyclists required. It was less exclusive and less political than the Irish Automobile Club became under the presidency of Sir Horace Plunkett. The A.A. established branches in Dublin, Cork and Belfast and the services it provided helped the man of modest means or limited mechanical enthusiasm to take to the roads confidently in his motor car. By 1910 Irish motorists were not over-sanguine in their conviction that 'the car had rooted itself in the category of the invincible ordinary', though an average car still cost between £200 and £800, whilst an early sixty h.p. Mercedes cost £2,500.[3] Ford's Model T, the famous 'Tin Lizzie,' brought motoring to the man of modest means in 1911, but the popular market for cheap standardised light cars was not adequately supplied until the 1920s, when car ownership became essential for people struggling for status.

Young woman with standardised bicycle which has an enclosed chain and all the usual comforts and accessories

The sense of liberation brought by cycling and motoring was in striking contrast to the awe in which the railways never ceased to be held. Steam locomotives' size, fierceness and difficulty of control; the rigidity of train time-tabling; and the fixity of the tracks, imposed an inflexible pattern on the movements of people and goods. The railways favoured some regions and towns, they by-passed others, they were owned and managed by companies which made vital decisions about times and frequency of trains, fares and freight rates in the interests of the profits of shareholders rather than the communities they served,[4] or so it was thought in Ireland in the first decades of the twentieth century when the monopoly of the railway companies seemed destined to last forever.[5] Above all they separated first-class from third-class passengers by segregating them into separate carriages and waiting-rooms. In Ireland there was an additional factor: the British Government took over control of the Irish railways on 1 January 1917 and did not hand them back to the companies until 17 August 1921. This meant that the railways were targets for strategic attacks during the Irish War of Independence[6] and the Irish and Ulster rebels quickly discovered the utility of motor transport or the added mobility that bicycles gave to a flying column.

Motoring like cycling was essentially a private, do-it-yourself kind of activity. Though motorists were not generally popular figures because of the dust they generated and the accidents they were alleged to cause, neither were they formidable ones as the aristocratic carriage-owners had been. Humour accompanied the motor car, its unpredictable temperament, and the necessary mechanical involvement.

Despite the excellent quality of Irish horses and the importance of horse-breeding and horse-transport in the economy,[7] the pioneers of the new mechanical forms of transport, both cycling and motoring—and they were frequently the same individuals—seem to have found Ireland a welcoming environment in contrast to the hostility which they had to suffer from the populace, the magistracy and the police in England.[8] The relatively low density of the population, the superficial impact of the railway system on Irish economic development, and the historic familiarity of the people with emigration and journeys are factors which contributed to this adaptability. There is a striking similarity between the French and Irish people's enthusiasm for the new sporting pastime which contrasts with the hostile conservatism it met with in England. This indicates that there were few socio-psychological deterrents impeding the adoption of innovations or inventions in transport in Ireland in the first quarter of the twentieth century. In fact the advent of the motor car, motor bus[9] and motor lorry was the culmination of a period of high investment and development of the Irish transport system.[10] The whole network of light railways in the remote districts had just been completed, tram tracks were laid in the cities,[11] and cyclists had taken to the roads.[12]

The traditional Irish value of hospitality had a new public who appreciated it: the early cycling and motor tourists. W. J. Duignan, the Walsall Liberal solicitor, who made fact-finding tours of Ireland between 1883 and 1884, chose to travel by road on his tricycle so that he might travel independently and talk to the people in their own homes. He commented: 'My mode of travel drove me a good deal into the cottages of the peasants, both for food and shelter . . . , and I may say here that a more courteous people I never

An 1899 'International' driven by the granddaughter of Charles Bianconi

Chambers body assembly shop, University Street, Belfast

travelled amongst.'[13] Charles Jarrot in his classic *Ten Years of Motors and Motor Racing 1896-1906* describes the Irish roads when automobiles were first challenging the dominance of the fast Irish horses drawing light carts: '. . . I do not think that I could ever recall a touring experience which gave me greater pleasure, which provided me with happier recollections and the sight of finer scenery than a tour I had in Ireland in 1901 . . . There was a blessed relief from the irksome, troublesome, and unjustifiable officialism of the police in England.' Members of the R.I.C. were not officious in enforcing the detail of the law about speed limits as they were in England. This, coupled with the increasingly chaotic state of law enforcement in Ireland during the period when motor transport was becoming common, probably contributed to the slap-happy nature of Irish motoring. This reputation persists. Herbert McCabe, the Dominican philosopher, writing of the necessity for agreed rules in society speaks of the excitement and challenge of getting by in a society where everyone makes up the rules as he goes. 'Those who have driven a car in Ireland' he says, 'will know what I mean.'

The good image of Ireland as a motorist's paradise was enhanced when the permission to hold the Gordon Bennett race in Ireland in 1903 was obtained after attempts to secure an English course had proved unsuccessful. This was the only occasion on which this great speed event was run in the British Isles. The 103 mile-long course was carefully prepared, the R.I.C. gave every assistance and the people were welcoming. The English, French, German and American competitors appreciated this opportunity to test and measure the performance of their cars.[14] At this time international races made a vital contribution towards perfecting the design and reliability of the automobile, so this was a milestone in the development of motoring in the British Isles. The Irish enthusiasm for the new sporting pastime encouraged the inventors and pioneers as did popular French support during the decade 1896–1906, that was crucial for the evolution of the standardised motor car. Because of the conservatism of automobile engineers and the rigidity imposed by methods of mass production, it is still based on the reciprocating internal combustion engine.

The sporting events familiarised the Irish people with the possibilities of motor transport at an early stage in its development, expanded the Irish market for cars and gave Irish mechanics good opportunities to develop the highest standard for this new trade. The foundations of the motor-car service industry were laid; in many cases cycle dealers' repair shops which spread a network over the country in the first decade of the twentieth century diversified into the motor trade.[15] By 1920 it was a fast growth industry creating employment for skilled and unskilled labour, which contributed to the reliability of motor transport and covered the country with garages supplying fuel. Chambers Motors Ltd began to build four-cylinder cars on a commercial basis in Belfast as early as 1907. They advertised as 'The only cars manufactured throughout in Ireland' adding the slogan 'Support Home Industries'. They built up a good reputation and continued manufacturing until 1927 when increased competition and assembly line production forced large numbers of independent manufacturers either to amalgamate or go out of business.

The Irish motor-engineering industry was given a great boost when the mighty Ford company built and equipped a first-class factory at Cork for the manufacture of agricultural tractors, which was completed in 1919. Henry Ford's decision was based on sentiment: 'My ancestors came from near

Cork and that city with its wonderful harbour has an abundance of fine industrial sites. We chose Ireland for a plant because we wanted to start Ireland along the road to industry.' However, that particular venture proved abortive. The plant was changed into a foundry to supply the Manchester plant.[16] It was one of the bases on which the motor-assembly industry was built, and it provided almost 2,000 jobs in the depressed city of Cork. J. B. Ferguson designed the 'Fergus' car and built a prototype in Belfast in 1911. His brother Harry built and raced his own motor-cycle and motor car and was the first Briton to design, build and fly his own aeroplane. But the Fergusons did not attract sufficient financial backing to support their inventive genius which was very effectively exploited in the more adventurous commercial climates of the United States and Britain. Ferguson's design was decisive in the evolution of the dependable low-cost tractor produced by Ford, which dominated the British Isles market until the end of the 1939–45 war. When he contracted out of the agreement with Ford, tractors designed by him in collaboration first with Standard Motors (U.K.) and later with the Canadian Massey-Harris concern, increased their share of the world market. [17]

The saddest story of lost manufacturing opportunity was the failure to exploit successfully in Ireland John Boyd Dunlop's invention of the pneumatic tyre in Belfast in 1889. The principle was not new but its re-discovery at this time was crucial for the evolution of both the chain-driven safety bicycle which became standardised by the end of the 1890s and of the automobile on which pneumatic tyres were first used in 1895, solving the problem of its weakest component. Dunlop was not an effective business man and lost control to Du Cros, a pioneering firm in the English motor business. For a short time the manufacturing of Dunlop tyres was carried on in Belfast and Dublin but the Dunlop Pneumatic Tyre Company soon moved to Coventry which was the original capital of the cycle industry, and in 1908 moved on to Birmingham which specialised in the production of cheap, reliable bicycles.[18] Cycles could be produced in any engineering centre, as innovation in the bicycle had come to an end in 1907 with the production of the 'Golden' Sunbeam Bicycle. Pierce & Company of Wexford and the Lucania Cycles and Engineering Works in Dublin were early Irish manufacturers of bicycles,[19] while later, Gordon Brothers of Hillsborough established themselves as manufacturers of about 700 custom-built racing-bicycles a year as a part of their

J. B. Dunlop riding his pneumatic-tyred bicycle

general blacksmith business.[20] But the economies of scale that could be achieved by the giant manufacturers of the English Midlands made it impossible for Irish manufacturers to retain the home market without some measure of protection. The protection policy pursued by the Free State in the thirties encouraged Raleigh to start production in Dublin, using tyres made in Cork. A sturdy bicycle suited to the Irish market was produced and about 50,000 bicycles were manufactured annually. The Government strengthened the protection which the motor-vehicle assembly industry had enjoyed since the inception of the state by a system of quotas on unassembled cars and lorries, body chassis, tyres and plugs. This industry not only created employment but trained large numbers of workers in light-engineering skill and stimulated the coach-building work and design carried on in the workshops of the major transport companies. It established the necessary infrastructure of skill and concentration of services on which more recent industrial enterprises have built.[21]

Whilst the cyclist has remained free of bureaucratic control, untaxed, unlicensed, uncounted, motorists have always been regulated. However, cyclists have had to suffer for this freedom through unfair treatment in legal proceedings, having their rights ignored in schemes of road planning or improvement, and finally, because of the bicycle's very cheapness and convenience as a form of private travel for those who could not afford motor cars, having to bear the discouraging stigma of a symbol of low social status.

The basic code which has governed Irish motoring was outlined in the Motor Car Act of 1903. Registration of motor vehicles and the carrying of number plates were made compulsory, drivers had to be licensed by the local authority in which they resided, but the only requirements were that they had reached seventeen years and could pay 5s; fourteen-year-olds could get a licence to drive motor-cycles. The speed limit was raised generally from fourteen to twenty miles per hour but it could be restricted by local authorities in the interest of the safety of the public to ten miles per hour in certain areas. In 1904 minimum standards of road-worthiness were laid down: cars should be able to reverse, have two brakes, carry a white light in front and a red light in the rear, have a horn, and be so constructed as to enable the driver to turn off the engine when the car was stationary, in order to prevent noise. In 1910 taxes were levied on motor vehicles in relation to their horse-power and on petrol. The net proceeds were to be disbursed to the local authorities to improve existing roads, or, subject to approval by the Road Board, to construct and maintain a limited section of new public highway. Special regulations were made for lorries and trailers: considerable powers were given to the local authorities to restrict the use of heavy vehicles on bridges for which they were responsible. This was a very necessary provision since, despite the clamour raised by motorists about the rough surface of Irish roads or the uneven standard of repair between one stretch and another, the network was adequate to meet the new traffic, except for the fragility and narrowness of some bridges, the congestion of certain urban streets and the fact that roads in scenic areas were mostly unmetalled.

The roads were there to be cycled or driven over; miles and miles of them, built with Grand Jury money or as toll roads in the eighteenth century, planned by the Board of Works in the nineteenth century, some meandering wherever a road was possible, due to desperate attempts to devise a public scheme on which men might work for necessary relief in famine times.[22] The surfaces were designed to meet the needs of fast, light horses drawing Irish cars, or herds of cattle on their way to fairs or railway stations. In the cities the tramway systems had pre-empted the central lanes of all the main thoroughfares and though this ensured that the surface was hard and solid, the congestion they caused was very inconvenient to all other road-users. The materials of which good roads are made—stone, labour, and constructional skill—were available in abundant quantities.[23] All that had to be imported were steam-rollers, so the return to the roads in Ireland did not create any immediate demand for large capital investment as the canal and railway innovations had. Irish roads were maintained at a relatively low cost.[24] Laws were framed to protect the interests of the traditional road-users and it seemed reasonable to conclude that the provisions of the Development and Road Improvement Funds Act of 1909 catered adequately for the additional wear and tear caused by motors. But it was quickly discovered that motorists' demands for road improvements were insatiable. Through their organisations they had devised an effective method of publicising their interests and exerting pressure on local and central government. The vehicles proved to be more useful than had been envisaged and the number and weight of road vehicles increased annually at a rate that exceeded even the sanguine expectations of the enthusiasts. Motorists had to be people of substance; they acted as if their tax contributions gave them a prior right to the use of highways of the standard

Chambers standard touring car (pre-1914)

they required, though in the years before 1914 contributions from the Road Fund amounted to approximately ten per cent of total expenditure on only the upkeep of the public highways.[25] Every road however good has its breaking point, and lack of maintenance between 1914 and 1923, coupled with an unexpected increase in heavy transport made the problem of repair urgent. In 1924 the Free State Government granted £1 million towards improvement of the road system, which in turn helped to make the roads more attractive.

The roads had never been deserted and in the last decade of the nineteenth century middle-class bicyclists pedalled along country roads, visiting, touring, racing, enjoying the fresh air, precursors of the industrial workers and country people who found the bicycle pre-eminent as a means of personal transport and for the local delivery of goods in the Irish environment. Cycling did not become general until the twenties when the price of a good bicycle dropped to around £5 and easy-payments schemes became general. During the fashionable period in the 1890s good safety bicycles had cost anything between £10 and £20 and tyres had cost as much as 15s. each. The advent of the motor car creamed off the upper-class cyclists so that it was primarily middle-class people who took to the road before men and who in more or less equal numbers, enjoying the exercise and the extended range the bicycle gave to their journeys. As they could afford season-tickets on the local trains, or houses in suburbs served by the tramway system, it does not appear that cycling was a decisive factor in the desertion by this class of city houses. But in the 1920s the bicycle freed the city labouring man from the need to find a dwelling within a mile's radius of his place of work, reinforcing the drift to the suburbs. New social horizons were opened also to the increasingly isolated dweller in the Irish countryside.

In 1911 there were 5,058 registered motor cars, buses and lorries and 4,111 motor-cycles. In the pioneering days no distinction was made between motor-cyclists and motor drivers; they were fellow-exploiters of the internal combustion engine. But with the standardisation of motor cars and the production of relatively cheap models such as the Ford, the numbers of motor-cycles did

Crossley 'Bullnose' lorry—1919 model—fitted with experimental armour—Dublin

not increase proportionately to that of other forms of motor transport. In that year there were cars registered in all the Irish counties. Leitrim and Longford had fewest with twenty-two and twenty-six respectively which reflects the relatively depressed condition of those counties. The 682 cars registered in Dublin were mainly used for private transport though already the maintenance and distribution side was well catered for by seventeen identifiable firms. In addition there were 753 cars registered in Dublin county. Though Belfast was a more populous and industrially-advanced city there were fewer registrations, 567, in the Belfast corporation area but here at least twelve per cent were owned by industrial concerns and twenty-six vehicles were registered separately as Heavy Motor Cars. This indicates that motoring in Dublin was primarily for private transport at this stage and that the retail trade was in the hands of Dublin distributors whilst in Belfast important steps had already been taken to use motors for freight and passenger transport. Doctors, priests and clergymen figure among the earliest users of motors, for their professional convenience no doubt, but their endorsement of 'the new thing' must have been an important factor in popularising motor transport in a society in which neither the landed class nor the bourgeoisie were regarded as acceptable leaders.

Road transport ideally suited Ireland's economic and social structure. The distances passengers or goods had to be carried were quite short, there was little demand for the regular transport of heavy goods between fixed terminals, the country was sparsely populated and the sectors of the cities devoted to cheaper dwellings were grossly over-crowded. The rail system was under-utilised except on certain passenger lines, though by the beginning of the twentieth century the railways had completely eclipsed the canals except for certain specialised goods.[26] The only brake on the success of the new mode of transport was the lack of means to own a car, lorry or indeed, bus. The convenient horse transport was severely affected by the compulsory re-quisitioning of horses for the front in 1914, a blow from which the hackney trade did not recover. The First World War and the War of Independence masked the inroads which had been made on the railways' passenger and goods traffic. The last quarter of the nineteenth century had been a period of heavy investment in inland and coastal water as well as rail transport.[27] The Dundalk, Newry and Greenore Railway backed by the powerful London North Western Railway Company initiated a heavy programme of investment which aimed at developing the potential of Greenore as a port and holiday centre. The Belfast and County Down Railway availed itself of a government grant to open a line to Ardglass in 1892 whilst investing heavily in the development of tourist potential of Newcastle. In 1906 the Great Northern Railway linked its mainline with Newcastle and in 1901 it extended a line from Armagh through Keady to Castleblaney. From 1883 government subsidies and baronial guarantees of interest encouraged the spread of a system of light railways and tramways in the remotest parts of the country. The Skibbereen to Schull tramway was opened in 1886, the West Clare Railway in 1887, the West Donegal system was completed in 1893, the line to Clifden in 1895. This government-sponsored investment, whilst it provided a useful social amenity for about a period of twenty years and contributed to the initial development of the tourist industry, did not yield the returns that were expected, and contributed to the deadweight of obsolescent fixed capital with which the Governments of Northern Ireland and of the Free State were burdened. Between 1894 and 1904 the Government disbursed almost one and half million pounds on projects of this type. Private or commercial road transport was flexible and cheap. Little capital was required to set up in the haulage business, in fact, it was more economic.

Though motor competition was already apparent before the First World War it did not prepare the railway and canal companies for the cut-throat competition with which they were faced by small independent lorry and bus

Mixed traffic in Patrick Street, Cork, in the 1920s

The first S/D freighter, used for transporting Guinness, 1927

owners on the resumption of peace. Independent bus companies and motor hauliers proliferated, helped by cheapness of ex-army vehicles, the facility of hire-purchase arrangements and the flexibility of an industry that was free from regulation. The ràtes for passengers and freight were very low due to the fierce competition amongst road-transporters who were themselves squeezed between entrepreneurial aspiration and fear of the growing spectre of unemployment. They indulged in savage competition for passengers, undercutting fares and racing with each other to stopping places and destinations whilst their vehicles were badly maintained and their employees paid erratically. The speed, cheapness and convenience of motor transport made an immediate appeal despite its chaotic organisation. It had its heyday before rationalisation was imposed. Though the independent bus companies did not survive, and control was imposed on road hauliers, it could no longer be said that rail was the dominant form of land transport in Ireland. Labouring people had bicycles, middle-income people owned motor cars, buses brought passengers and goods to the door-step and a new level of expectation of transport services had emerged in which the railways at best might provide an important link in a chain of complementary coverage. The experience of the twenties demonstrated that they could not survive in open competition with road transport. In the 1930s dividends were not paid and the price of railway stock fell dramatically. The national interest was the only rational argument for their conservation, and the rescue of some of the fixed capital assets which the railways represented ultimately entailed nationalisation of the public transport systems both north and south to avert closure.[28] The really dramatic increase in car ownership did not appear until after the Second World War.[29]

Of the many social and economic consequences of the return to the roads—the elimination of the upper-class monopoly of comfortable, flexible transport; the blurring of boundaries between town and country; the increased expedition of business and journeys; the relative reduction in cost; the alteration in marketing and retail patterns; the development of new industries and new industrial locations; the alteration in the scale and intensity of warfare—I would like to comment on two. Whereas Ireland was always at a disadvantage in the railway age due to her geography and economic structure, this disadvantage has been neutralised as, in common with other European countries, she is now dependent on oil imports but at least has the heritage of a comprehensive road-system and the natural resources to maintain her roads, while low density of population makes the motor age more enjoyable and more profitable in Ireland than in more densely-populated, traditionally industrialised regions. Secondly, cycling or driving is an active rather than a passive occupation; to do either safely demands alertness, judgement, precision, boldness and awareness of a complicated environment. It was in these ways that science and technology impinged most directly on Irish society. The roads brought a new sense of emancipation and at the same time they demanded discipline, concentration and a certain respect for laws and rules in their use. The return to the roads was on new terms.

11 The Latest Phase in Irish Transport

Gerard Quinn and Patrick Lynch

THE NINETEENTH century was the period of major rail development in Ireland. The peak of railway prosperity occurred during the First World War. However, the war also marked a decisive turning-point for the railways. It provided a minor boom before a period of increasing and incessant difficulty which has lasted until the present time.

After the war the rapid expansion of motor transport provided the railways with a measure of competition which they had not faced before. They were also burdened with a heavy increase in their major cost—labour. Labour costs had risen to nearly three times their pre-war level and the 1920s was therefore a period of growing crisis for the Irish railways.

In an attempt to combat these difficulties, twenty-six separate railway companies amalgamated and formed the Great Southern Railway Company which was established in January 1925, with a capital of approximately £26 million. However, centralised control and combined operation could not redress the problems from which the railways suffered. It should be remembered that the rail network had been constructed in the nineteenth century to serve a far greater population than now existed. Moreover the increasing gravitation of the population towards the eastern part of the country was depriving many of the rural lines of business. But an even greater threat to the railways at this time was the diversion of passenger traffic and freight to the roads. The railways were not empowered to own or to operate road transport services until 1927, when they were allowed to do so in an attempt to offset growing road competition. Private road haulage and passenger companies also enjoyed the advantage that they were not subject to regulations governing their fares, routes or regularity of services They were thus far better equipped to plan their operations to suit the varying requirements of different areas than was the nation-wide rail system. These advantages helped to give the private road operators an increasing hold, especially over short-distance traffic.

In 1932 legislation was introduced to control the private road passenger services. A system of licensing was adopted to limit new entrants. No new licences were to be issued except in clear case of need. Regularity of services had to be provided; timetables and fare lists had to be published. The weak financial position of the railways was also helped by the Railways Act of 1933, under which the capital of Great Southern Railway was reduced from £26 million to £12·4 million. This meant that a sum of £13·6 million was written off, a severe blow to those who held investments in the formerly high-grade and safe rail shares, because this represented a real loss to shareholders, not a mere book-entry.

In 1933 two further Acts were passed which provided the basis of subsequent national transport policy. The prime objective was to redress the financial position of the railways and to provide firm safeguards against road competition.

The Road Transport Act of 1933 stiffened the regulations controlling the private road companies. Their area of operation and class of merchandise to

Loco No. 5 of the former West Clare Railway. This engine worked on the narrow-gauge West Clare Section until dieselisation in 1952

Diesel railcar set on West Clare Railway

be carried were here defined and limited. The 1933 Act also gave to the railways the power of compulsory acquisition of the licences of the private operators. This right was exercised to a substantial extent, and effectively eliminated the private road companies. It meant that the Great Southern Railways had, by the outbreak of the Second World War, an almost complete monopoly of road passenger services outside Dublin, and the company had also acquired a very large share of road freight business as well. However, the railways did not get all the extra business they might reasonably have expected from taking over their rivals at high prices. It was not uncommon for the former private licence-holder to begin to trade himself in the commodities which he had formerly transported for reward—and carriage by a trader of his own goods remained unaffected by the regulations. A pertinent illustration, perhaps, of the resilience of the free-enterprise spirit in the face of state intervention!

The 1933 legislation marked a decisive stage in the evolution of the Government's transport policy. In the 1930s the chief problem was the mushroom growth of small-scale private operators who had an eye to profits rather than community service. The 1933 legislation sounded their general death-knell.

It was perhaps a pity that the implications of imposing a social as well as an economic function on the nation's transport services were not explicitly accepted by the Government. The rail companies were expected to pay their way fully while carrying the albatross of socially desirable but loss-incurring lines around their necks. Here lay the origin of a dilemma which was to pose the greatest problem in the future.

Despite the various measures of assistance, the finances of the G.S.R. continued to decline in the 1930s. The railways were severely affected in this period by the impact of the economic war with Britain and by the general slump in trade during the depression years. Both these influences had serious repercussions on the volume of freight business. There was a particularly sharp decline in the number of livestock carried on the railways. Little or no return was earned on capital. The company did not manage even to maintain adequately its rolling stock or track, quite apart from the increasingly urgent task of modernisation. Many of the smaller western lines were closed down and by 1938 the net revenues from the railways were at their lowest level since 1922.

The extent of the financial deterioration of the railways is shown by the fact that both revenue and expenditure declined by approximately one quarter between 1925 and 1938.

The persistence of the problems, despite the efforts made by amalgamation, reorganisation and restrictions on private road competition, led to the setting up of a Tribunal of Inquiry on Public Transport in December 1938. This Tribunal made a number of recommendations including: further restrictions on motor vehicles other than those operated by the statutory transport companies; a pooling of passenger traffic between the G.S.R. and the Dublin

An early Belfast–Dublin Enterprise Express

Mainline express train at Killiney, Co. Dublin

United Tramway Company; and a recommendation that the borrowing power of the G.S.R. should be increased.

However, this Tribunal in its report really evaded the fundamental issue of the over-extension of the rail network and the incessant financial drag of heavily uneconomic lines. The Great Southern Railway Company itself did not have any such inhibitions. In evidence to the Tribunal, the company recommended a wholesale closure of uneconomic lines, which would have involved the closing down of about thirty-seven per cent of the country's total rail system. Replacement of its major loss (by running branch lines by alternative forms of transport), as well as being an important benefit to the company's current earnings position, would also lessen the burden of the onerous capital replacement and modernisation programme.

However, the Tribunal evaded this controversial proposal. It contented itself with remarking that a much more detailed study was needed and that the company's proposals about closures were at that time 'acceptable only in a general sense'.

The outbreak of war provided the railways with a temporary respite. The restrictions on private transport diverted traffic to the railways. Railway rates and fares were increased which helped revenue, while wage increases were restricted by the emergency controls. However, it was always clear that this respite would be purely temporary and that the deep-rooted problems of the railways would reassert themselves again, once the war was over.

In 1942 an Emergency Powers Order was enacted which enabled the Government to appoint the Chairman of the G.S.R. with four Directors to be elected by the shareholders. The Transport Act of 1944 followed. This Act provided for the merger of the Great Southern Railway and the Dublin United Tramway Company into a new organisation, Córas Iompair Éireann. The new company quickly ran into difficulties after the war. It was affected by the resumption of wage increases, the renewal of road competition and an increase in coal prices.

The growing financial problems of C.I.E. led the Coalition Government in 1948 to appoint an expert Committee to examine the problems of Irish transport, under the Chairmanship of the British rail expert, Sir John Milne. The Milne Report, issued in 1949, fully recognised some of the basic problems affecting C.I.E.: the need for a major capital replacement programme; heavy maintenance costs; management and organisational problems arising from the merger of two quite different organisations.

However, the criticism may be made that Milne failed to strike at the basic root of the problem, although he defined the essential features of it. There was in Ireland an unusually extensive network of roads and railways in relation to the size and the population of the country. Yet the extent of travel per head of population in Ireland was the lowest in Europe; and the proportion of rail seating capacity used was also among the lowest in Europe.

The railway system was subjected to steadily increasing pressure of competition from the roads. Whether, in the light of all this, it made economic or social sense to maintain the over-extended rail network, including heavily uneconomic lines, was an issue that had to be faced.

In the late 1940s there was a continued deterioration in the finances of the railways, caused mainly by a large decline in the freight of commodities such as livestock and coal. The slump in coal freight—which provided three-fifths of total rail receipts—was caused mainly by the diversion of this business to road transport. There was also a substantial fall in the number of passengers carried by rail as between pre- and post-war. A good part of this fall represented a shift from rail services to C.I.E. road services. However, much of it

C.I.E. suburban train crossing the Loopline Bridge en route from Connolly Station, Dublin

was also attributable to the large increase in the number of private motor cars. Between 1938 and 1950 the number of private motor cars had increased from approximately 48,600 to over 85,000—an increase of just over three-quarters.

The position was brighter in the road section of C.I.E.'s operations. On its road services, growth in revenue kept pace with growth in expenditure, through a combination of a rise in passenger numbers and a rise in fares. But there was a considerable discrepancy between the city bus services which were operating economically and those in rural areas where quite a contrary trend was in evidence.

The Great Northern Railway also found itself facing many difficulties. After 1922 the G.N.R. was operating in two separate political areas with the Border intersecting its lines at various points. Because of its dual location the G.N.R. was excluded from the amalgamation of rail companies which took place under the 1924 Act. Although it had managed to operate at a profit during the war, it encountered severe competition after the war from the publicly-owned Ulster Transport Authority. While it was managing to show a profit on its operations in the Republic the position was reversed in the Six Counties. The situation was ripe for nationalisation of the company. In 1950 discussions between the Southern and Northern Governments resulted in the joint acquisition of the G.N.R. in 1953 for £4·5 million. In September of that same year a Board was set up to manage the undertaking jointly on behalf of both Governments.

This arrangement did not, however, resolve the Great Northern's problems and some 149 miles of the Board's system in Northern Ireland had to be closed to traffic. In the first five years of the Board's existence losses were severe and so a new agreement was made between the two Governments in September 1958. As a result of this arrangement, the Great Northern Board was dissolved and the line south of the border brought under the control of C.I.E. and in the north under that of the Ulster Transport Authority, with the two undertakings running the services between Dublin and Belfast. In Northern Ireland, the U.T.A., which had been established in 1948, became the only public transport authority apart from the municipal services provided by Belfast Corporation and under the terms of the 1962 Northern Ireland Transport Act, provision was made for parliamentary grants to the authority of up to £4 million.

In the Republic, the Transport Act of 1950 which followed the Milne Report, established the principle of state ownership over the railways. C.I.E. was amalgamated with the Grand Canal Company. The 1950 Act imposed a duty on the Board of the reorganised C.I.E. of securing as soon as possible that, taking one year with another, the revenue of the Board shall not be less than sufficient to meet the charges properly chargeable to revenue.

However, the underlying structural problems and the adverse impact of changed travel habits remained as keen as ever. The fleet of approximately 400 locomotives was over fifty years of age on average, while the 680 passenger coaches were also approaching the half-century mark. The Board was confronted with a major modernisation programme as an immediate necessity. However, it was not until 1953 that such a programme was approved by the Government. It provided for an almost complete change-over from steam to diesel engines, and for renewal of a considerable portion of the carriages, at an estimated cost of £11·65 million.

The experience of the railways in this period from the early 1930s up to the early 1950s is illustrative of certain basic conflicts. First, was the conflict between social and strictly commercial considerations in the operation of a national railway service. Secondly, the period illustrates the economic pressures confronting the railways because of steadily growing competition from private road companies, and the increasing habit of private road travel. It provides a case study as well of the gradual transference of a national enterprise from widespread private ownership into a monopoly state concern.

To turn briefly to a consideration of the roadways, the new state faced an exceptionally heavy burden of road improvement and extension. Roads had been comparatively neglected in the early part of the century when the railways were still flourishing. With the growth of the private motor car and commercial road traffic, attention began to be paid to the road network. In 1909 a separate Road Fund was set up; finance from motor taxes was paid into this fund and allocated to road improvements.

However, the intervention of war halted the necessary work of catching up with a huge backlog of road neglect, and when the war was over, the problem was considerably greater. It was compounded by the rapid acceleration in the volume of motor traffic after the war, as well as by the faster speeds which increased the burden of road maintenance.

The Irish Government turned with commendable energy to tackling this serious problem. In 1926 a national road scheme involving £2 million was adopted. It was completed by 1930, when the state had 5,000 miles of paved road surfaces. The work of improvement continued throughout the thirties with expenditure of about £1 million per year. It was in this period of the latter thirties that many major projects, such as the dual carriageway linking Dublin and Bray, were carried out. It is interesting to note that this particular project, like so many others at the time, was criticised as being prohibitively expensive, a criticism which seems in hindsight somewhat grotesque.

By 1940 the paved roadways of the state had been extended to 11,000 miles, and the worst of the drastic condition of neglect which existed in the early 1920s had been overcome. During the second war, shortages of capital, equipment and materials brought the work of improvement to a temporary standstill, and work was largely confined to essential upkeep. For five years after the war, work was devoted mainly to making good the dilapidations caused by lack of repair work and general neglect of the roads during the war. Still, by 1950 the paved road surface had been extended to over 14,000 miles.

A brief mention may be made of the major initiatives in this period affecting Ireland's external communications. Aer Lingus, the national airline, was formed in May 1936. Initially its operations were on an extremely small scale, especially in the war years, but from the end of the war a rapid expansion occurred in its operations. An Agreement was signed between the British and Irish Governments in April 1946, which gave Aer Lingus the sole right to carry passengers between the two countries on scheduled passenger flights. This Agreement also provided for a share participation by B.O.A.C. and B.E.A. in the Irish Company.

Aer Lingus's first aircraft which had its maiden flight in 1936

In February 1947 Aerlínte was established to undertake transatlantic services. However, in view of the increasingly unfavourable financial situation, the Government decided not to proceed with this venture at that particular time. In 1951 the question was again examined, but again came to nothing because the American Civil Aeronautics Board was willing only to enter on an Agreement limited to two years. It was not until a later period that the most profitable branch of the Irish airline's business, namely its operation on transatlantic routes, was to be established.

Another landmark was the establishment of the customs-free airport at Shannon in 1947. This was the first customs-free airport in the world, and the decision to proceed with it was based on the contribution made in many countries by customs-free seaports. The objective was to offset the increasing danger of Shannon being by-passed by longer-haul jet aircraft which were able to travel much greater distances than before without re-fuelling. It was hoped to attract a significant volume of air freight business inwards and outwards with Shannon acting as a major entrepôt and distribution centre for Europe, and attracting manufacturing plants to the area because of the duty concessions. This was an imaginative and original concept at the time, and it has in the interval fulfilled many of the hopes originally reposed in it.

During the war the Irish Government also decided to set up Irish Shipping as a Statutory Company with the objective of maintaining the flow of essential materials. Aer Lingus and Irish Shipping were major initiatives by the Government in the commercial field. However, the motivation in setting up these semi-state concerns was certainly not the earning of a commercial profit—although this possibility was not discounted—but rather to bring Ireland into the forefront of international communications. These ventures provided sea and air access under national control, a particularly important consideration for an island country on the perimeter of a continent. Had the state not done so, there was no prospect at all that private enterprise would have filled the gap, in view of the very heavy capital requirements and the extremely limited prospect of earning a commercial return on the capital investment involved.

In 1950 the Republic was entering a decade, most of which was to be disappointing for social and economic policy. The Transport Act of 1950 had amalgamated the Grand Canal Company with Córas Iompair Éireann, but no one had high hopes that that Act would dispose of the cheerless legacy which C.I.E. had inherited from a history not always of its own making.

There was to be yet another investigation into the problems of Irish internal public surface transport, and so in July 1956, the Beddy Committee was set up.

Its report reflected the spirit of despondency in Ireland in 1957. It attached particular importance to the employment content of the railways, however low their productivity, although the Committee was opposed to subsidies for the railways. One of its key recommendations was a truly sibylline one: the Committee saw no reason for the continuance of the railway system as it was then constituted and operated; on the other hand the Committee was not satisfied that 'under changed circumstances the railways would fail to justify their existence'. In short, the railways were to be reprieved for a limited number of years to prove themselves.

After the report of the Beddy Committee the Transport Act of 1958 was passed. It imposed on C.I.E. the duty of providing reasonable, efficient and economic transport services with due regard to safety, reasonable conditions of employment for staff and the encouragement of economic development nationally. This emphasis on the role of transport in economic development should be noted, since 1958 was the year in which the tide of economic depression was beginning to recede.

Following the publication of the First Programme for Economic Development and Dr Whitaker's document *Economic Development*, hopes were raised for the first time for over a decade that now at last a new era of Irish economic progress might be opening. C.I.E. however was not able to achieve the financial aim of the 1958 Act and break-even by March 1964. In that year there was another Transport Act which explicitly recognised the distinction between the commercial and social responsibilities of the company. There were certain operations which might not be directly commercial but which were essential for social purposes. C.I.E. would be paid a subsidy for these. It was arranged in 1969 that an annual grant of £2,650,000 would be payable to C.I.E. for such services over the subsequent five years. In 1971, however, the railway system and its problems were being investigated by a firm of industrial consultants. The outlook for the railways was dim for those who judged profit and loss by criteria other than those normally adopted by private commercial enterprise. But there was reason to believe that the Department of Transport and Power was anxious to employ modern econ-

A DC3 of the 1940s

omic techniques, such as cost-benefit analysis, to decide how far the railway system or parts of it provided social benefits which could not be measured by private commercial criteria.

In Northern Ireland, too, increased competition from road transport led to a steady decline in the prosperity of the railways. The substantial road mileage in relation to the limited area of Northern Ireland helped this movement away from the railways to the roads and private vehicles, and by 1965 of the 754 miles of railway which had been in service in 1920 only 297 miles were still open to traffic.

The continued financial problems facing the public transport undertaking, U.T.A. prompted the Northern Ireland Government, under the Transport Act of 1966, to abolish the U.T.A.'s monopoly of the public carriage of goods by road and to permit licensed carriers to operate. By the end of December 1969, some 1,880 such licences had been issued. Under the 1967 Transport Act, further steps were taken to dismantle the U.T.A. by putting the majority of the public bus services under the management of Ulsterbus Limited, while from 1968 onwards the Northern Ireland Railway Company has been responsible for the remaining railway services with provision for state aid towards capital outlay.

In the south at the beginning of the 1950s Aer Rianta Teoranta was a public limited liability company set up by the Government under the Companies

Acts to be responsible for civil aviation. It owned sixty per cent of the share capital in Aer Lingus which operated European services, and all the share capital in Aerlínte Éireann, the transatlantic company. The balance of the share capital in Aer Lingus—forty per cent—was at that time owned by British European Airways, an arrangement which continued until 1964 when Aer Lingus became wholly owned by the Irish community as a public enterprise.

The main Aer Lingus routes in the early 1950s were those from Dublin to London and Dublin to Paris. Services were gradually and successively extended to other English and Scottish cities and to Rome, Amsterdam, Zurich, Copenhagen, Frankfurt and elsewhere in Europe, especially with the first Viscount aircraft which began to replace the famous DC-3s after 1954. The DC-3s, two-engined Dakotas, were among the most successful aircraft ever built. They held their own until Vickers produced the famous Viscount designed by Sir George Edwards O.M., the turbo-prop aircraft which dominated the airline industry for more than a decade and established the commercial success of many airlines.

In the early 1950s Aer Lingus made heavy financial losses which were carried forward and made good out of later projects. During the decade 1950–60 Aer Lingus revenue was rising at an annual average rate of just over fifteen per cent. At the beginning of the 1950s total revenue had been just over £1 million a year. By 1960 it had increased to nearly £4 million a year.

In 1956 Aer Lingus entered a new phase following the revision of the Bilateral Agreement of 1946 between the Irish and British Governments. As a result Aer Lingus ceased to be the sole carrier from Dublin to Britain. British European Airways retained a ten per cent sharehold interest in Aer Lingus which was not relinquished until March 1964.

In 1961 Aer Lingus celebrated its twenty-fifth birthday. In that year too its sister company, Aerlínte Eireann, was operating the first of the Boeing 707 jet aircraft, the most modern aircraft available, acquired in December 1960 for the Atlantic route to replace the Super-Constellations which had been leased from Seaboard and Western Airlines since Aerlínte began transatlantic operations in 1958. The Super-Constellations were great aircraft; they were the last of the pre-jet generation. Being able to lease aircraft for these two years the Irish airline avoided capital expenditure on aircraft such as Super-Constellations, which would obviously have had a short life on the route.

A Boeing 707

In its European and Atlantic services the Irish airline formed, for operational purposes, a joint organisation with a common management. Fully integrated they became known as Aer Lingus Irish. There is a one-plane service from Dublin to Shannon and to New York, Boston, Montreal and Chicago. This arrangement was found satisfactory because a majority of passengers from the United States to Ireland wish to end their flight at Shannon. From Shannon in both directions east and west Aer Lingus Irish is in direct competition with the world's leading airlines.

An airline with routes as short as most of the European routes of Aer Lingus—on which the average fare is low and there are marked seasonal variations in the volume of passengers carried—must experience economic difficulty in trying to survive without state assistance. Aer Lingus did not receive direct subvention from the state although, like C.I.E., it was undoubtedly contributing to national economic development and to tourist promotion which might not otherwise have taken place.

In the case of Aerlínte, leased piston-engined Constellation aircraft were still being used until December 1960 when the first of three Boeings, the most up-to-date jet aircraft, went into service. The high speed of these jet aircraft reduced the time for the transatlantic flight by half and increased the passenger's comfort, as these aircraft fly at great heights above bad weather, thus avoiding most turbulent air conditions. In 1960–61, traffic was fifty-one per cent higher than in the previous year. The average fare fell by about four per cent. The airline's share of total air traffic between Ireland and North America continued to rise. Shannon Airport was unique in its location, achievement and potential. It provided immensely generous facilities to airlines of every other country, offering them freedom to put down and take up passengers and cargo for any destination. Under rights from the U.S. Government Aer Lingus Irish was restricted to serving only three American cities, New York, Boston and Chicago. It competed with three United States carriers and over a dozen European carriers serving Ireland; quite a challenge; not a bad achievement.

By the middle 1960s the operating profits of Aer Lingus Irish were amounting to over £1,250,000 a year after full provision had been made for depreciation. The bulk of this profit was earned by the transatlantic company, but European business was playing an increasingly useful part as a shorthaul feeder service. The gross revenue of the two companies amounted to £15 million. Seven years earlier it had been just under £5 million.

By 1970 the airline had become the largest exporting firm in the country, yet it had received no grant of any kind in the thirty-four years of its existence,

An Aerlínte Éireann Constellation

and received no subsidy since 1950. The Exchequer of course was its main shareholder. If, however, the airline had been a private firm exporting goods it would have been eligible for millions of pounds in grants towards building, machinery, training and adaptation. The airline gave employment directly to over 5,000 persons. Up to 1969 the state had invested £13.6 million of equity capital in it and, being the only shareholder, owned an asset which was worth much more than its nominal capital. No money dividends had been paid on this investment because the capital needed for rapid expansion of the airline had been such that profits were re-invested in the airline. Over the twenty years since 1950 the profit record of the airline as a whole was good in comparison with that of the other airlines of the world.

In the five year period ending March 1973 the capital expenditure of the airline would be of the order of £71 million. Of this sum the airline itself would provide £29 million from its own resources. Twenty-seven million pounds would be borrowed abroad at commercial rates of interest. The Oireachtas decided to increase the community investment in the airlines by £15 million. This represented an increase in the state equity holding of £10 million. In this way the airline was able to enter the seventies with a sound capital structure. As community-owned public utilities, Aer Lingus and C.I.E. have much in common, including their indirect economic and social returns, which do not appear in their commercial annual accounts.

In March 1963 there was an interesting and specific example of the kind of operation which state-sponsored enterprises may be expected to perform to produce those broader economic returns that appear in the national income accounts but not in the commercial accounts of the enterprise itself. The Government requested Aer Lingus to undertake a car-ferry service to give critical aid to the promotion of the tourist industry. This was an operation which Aer Lingus on its own initiative would not have introduced because neither then nor since is there an aircraft fully suitable for economic use as a car-ferry on the particular routes available to Aer Lingus. Nevertheless Aer Lingus initiated the service to Britain and France. The services proved to be extremely popular. They carried to Ireland many British and Continental motorists and their families and also enabled Irish motorists to take their cars quickly and at reasonable cost abroad. They added a new dimension to the Irish tourist industry. But the operation involved a continuous loss to the airline because fares high enough to be economic would have deterred motorists from using the service. And so it was with no reluctance that the air-ferry was withdrawn when a suitably equipped shipping service entered the car-ferry business. But such is the role of a state-sponsored enterprise, even a commercial one.

Within the general structure of the United Kingdom's air transport system, Northern Ireland, through its main airport, Aldergrove, has important facilities in terms of passenger and freight services which provide regular links with centres such as London, Glasgow, Prestwick and Shannon.

In 1964 British Rail introduced car-ferry services and by 1968 was operating from Holyhead and Dún Laoghaire and Fishguard and Rosslare. The British and Irish Steam Packet Company Limited was acquired by the Irish Government in 1965, a step that had long been urged by those who believed that, as an island, Ireland should control through a community-owned public enterprise some part of the surface traffic with Great Britain, its most important and nearest trading partner. The new B + I introduced services between Dublin and Liverpool and between Cork and Swansea which have been popular and successful.

Another spectacular feature of transport in the 1960s was the development of container services by the B + I and its principal competitor, British Rail, which introduced 'Freightliner' services between Dublin, London and Birmingham in 1968. In Northern Ireland, too, container and drive-on

The B+I MV 'Munster' car ferry introduced in 1968

B+I 'Freightway' door-to-door container service introduced in 1968

drive-off services have helped to facilitate trade with Britain and more distant markets—Belfast alone handling a container traffic of some 1·6 million tons per year.

The introduction of the container service met with considerable opposition, but it was eventually accepted that radical modernisation of sea transport services was inevitable if it were to survive in modern conditions. This modernisation soon took place. New needs were sought out and catered for: the man with his car, the container service for goods or, following the change in the character of Irish meat exports, insulation and refrigeration. Traditional structures in transport firms were broken down and new techniques adopted. This was a radical departure from old-fashioned ways by which individual cargo items were carried separately. They could now be carried in bulk. All this required heavy capital expenditure. B + I, in accordance with its objective, was providing and developing 'a modern, efficient and profitable national comprehensive cross-Channel surface transport system—to provide services for passengers, motor cars, live-stock and freight.

At the opening of the 1970s the future of Irish Shipping Limited was not clearly defined. Its long-term plans might most successfully be realised by a co-ordination with those of the B + I and C.I.E.

The prospect of Ireland entering the E.E.C. raised new problems because of the negative approach of the Treaty of Rome to transport. In 1971, however, a further rationalisation of internal transport seemed inevitable and it will be of interest to see the social role of the railways in this exercise.

Notes and Bibliographies

Chapter 1

1. See J. G. D. Clark, *Prehistoric Europe, the Economic Basis,* London 1965, 282–315.
V. G. Childe, *Piecing together the Past,* London 1956, 50–1.
Ibid., 163.
2. V. G. Childe, *Antiquity 32,* (1958), 69–74.
3. R. de Valera, *Proc. Roy. Ir. Acad. 60C,* (1960), 107–8.
H. O'N. Hencken, *Jnl. Roy. Soc. Antiq. Ire. 69,* (1939), 53–98.
Current Archaeology 2, (1970), 300–3.
4. H. L. Movius, *The Irish Stone Age,* Cambridge 1942, 91.
5. E. M. Jope, *Ulster Jnl. Arch. 15,* (1952), 31–50.
E. Rynne, *Jnl. Kildare Arch. Soc. 14,* (1964–5), 50–3.
6. J. Raftery, *Oibre 4,* (1966), 11–13.
W. R. Wilde, *A Descriptive Catalogue of the Antiquities in the Museum of the Royal Irish Academy,* Dublin 1863, 48–9.
R. J. Griffith, *Proc. Roy. Ir. Acad. 2,* (1840–4), 312–316; the plan and section reproduced on p. 14 probably came to the Academy about the same time as the material presented by Griffith (Antiquarian Portfolio I, f.8); the writer thanks the Council of the Royal Irish Academy for permission to publish photographs of these records.
7. S. P. O Riordain, *Antiquities of the Irish Countryside,* London 1952, 66–71.
S. Piggott, *Neolithic Cultures of the British Isles,* Cambridge 1954, 193–222.
S. P. O Riordain and G. E. Daniel, *New Grange and the Bend in the Boyne,* London 1964, 91–153.
8. K. Jessen, *Proc. Roy. Ir. Acad. 52B,* (1949), 99, 260.
9. M. Herity, *Irish University Review 1,* (1971), 258–265.
10. M. Herity in J. Filip. ed., *Actes du VIIe Congrès International Préhistoriques et Protohistoriques,* Praha 1970, 530–4.
M. Herity in *The Early Prehistoric Period around the Irish Sea,* Cardiff, ed. D. Moore, 1970, 33.
11. G. Coffey, *The Bronze Age,* Dublin and London 1913, 55.

J. H. Craw, *Proc. Soc. Antiq. Scotland 63*, (1928–9), 154, 89.

J. Taylor, *Proc. Preh. Soc. 36*, (1970), 38–81.

12. S. Piggott, *Proc. Preh. Soc. 34* (1968), 266–318.

13. F. Elrington Ball, *J.R.S.A.I. 43*, (1913), 276.

14. J. Van der Waals, *Prehistoric Disc Wheels in the Netherlands*, Groningen 1964.

15. J. Coles and F. A. Hibbert, *Proc. Preh. Soc. 34*, (1968), 238–58.

J. Coles and F. A. Hibbert, *Proc Preh. Soc. 36*, (1970), 125–51.

16. W. R. Wilde, *A Descriptive Catalogue of the Antiquities in the Museum of the Royal Irish Academy*, Dublin 1863, 251–4.

17. P. Tohall, Hl. de Vries and W. van Zeist, *J. R. S. A. I. 85*, (1955), 77–83; a corrected version of this radiocarbon date (1640 ± 170 B.C.) is given in a discussion of trackways in Littleton Bog, Co. Tipperary by E. Rynne, *North Munster Antiquarian Jnl. 7*, (1965), 138–42.

The brief account by J. K. Millner of the structure near Robertstown, Co. Kildare, suggests a trackway of similar construction in ten feet of bog, *J. R. S. A. I. 39*, (1909), 93.

18. J. Brondsted, *Danmarks Oldtid II*. Copenhagen 1939, 89.

19. S. P. O Riordain, 'A Burial with Faience Beads at Tara'; *Proc. Preh. Soc. 21*, (1955), 163–73.

20. S. Piggott, 'The Early Bronze Age in Wessex', *Proc. Preh. Soc. 4*, (1938), 52–106.

21. V. G. Childe, *Prehistoric Communities of the British Isles*, London 1940, 91–162.

D. L. Clarke, *Beaker Pottery of Great Britain and Ireland*, Cambridge 1970.

22. J. J. Butler, 'Bronze Age Connections across the North Sea', *Palaeohistoria 9*, (1963), 1–286.

23. G. Eogan, 'The Later Bronze Age in Ireland in the light of recent research', *Proc. Preh. Soc. 30*, (1964), 268–351.

24. However, Mr Barry Raftery has recently found traces of a circular timber-built house dating to the end of the Late Bronze Age (*c.* 700 B.C.), in excavations at Rathgall, Co. Wicklow.

25. G. Eogan, 'Lock-rings of the Late Bronze Age', [*Catalogue of Irish Bronze Swords*, Dublin 1965.] *Proc. Roy. Ir. Acad. 67C*, (1969), 97.

26. T. Pownall, 'An Account of some Irish Antiquities', *Archaeologia 3*, (1775), 368.

J. N. A. Wallace, 'The Golden Bog of Allen', *North Munster Antiquarian Journal 1*, (1936–9), 89–101.

M. Herity, 'Early Finds of Irish Antiquities', *Antiquaries Journal 49*, (1969), 1–21.

27. MacWhite lists twenty-nine occurrences of amber in 'Amber in the Irish Bronze Age', *Journal Cork Arch. and Hist.Soc. 49*, (1944), 122–7; finds as massive as the Whitegate one were made at Cullinagh Bog, Co. Cavan, and near Cong, Co. Mayo.

28. H. O'N. Hencken, 'Ballinderry crannóg no. 2', *Proc. Roy. Ir. Acad. 47C*, (1941) 8–9, Pl.II.

J. G. D. Clark, *Prehistoric Europe, the Economic Basis*, London 1952, 156–7.

29. The sites of Corlona and Robertstown are mentioned above (n17). Macalister

lists other roadways near Clonmacnoise, Co. Offaly, Monavallagh Bog, Co. Kildare, Duncan's flow, Co. Antrim and Cargahoge, Co. Monaghan; he later described another at Baltigeer, Co. Meath. Rynne has described three in Littleton Bog, near Thurles, Co. Tipperary; an earlier record of a trackway in this bog is given by D. McEvoy in *J. R. S. A. I. 3*, (1854–5), 132.

30. J. G. D. Clark, *Prehistoric Europe, the Economic Basis*, London 1952, 277 discusses the archaeological and literary evidence for Atlantic trade in the few centuries B.C. Ptolemy's map of Ireland is discussed by H. Bradley, 'Remarks on Ptolemy's Geography of the British Isles', *Archaeologia 48*, (1884), 379 and G. H. Orpen, 'Ptolemy's Map of Ireland', *J. R. S. A. I. 24*, (1894), 115.

31. Co. Roscommon, Ordnance Survey Six-Inch Sheet 21, 22; Co. Meath, Ordnance Survey Six-Inch Sheet 31.
R. A. S. Macalister, *Tara, A Pagan Sanctuary in Ancient Ireland*, London 1931, 60–9.

32. R. A. S. Macalister, *The Archaeology of Ireland*, Dublin 1928, 149–50.

33. S. P. O Riordain, 'Roman Material in Ireland', *Proc. Roy. Ir. Acad. 51C*, (1946), 35–82.

34. W. G. Wood-Martin, *The Lake-Dwellings of Ireland*, Dublin and London 1886, 237.
H. O'N. Hencken, 'Lagore crannóg', *Proc. Roy. Ir. Acad. 53C*, (1949), 115–6.

Chapter 2

BIBLIOGRAPHY

David Greene, 'The Chariot as described in Irish literature', *The Iron Age in the Irish Sea Province* (Council for British Archaeology Research Report 9), ed. C. Thomas, 1972.
Maire and Liam de Paor, *Early Christian Ireland*, London 1958.
J. O'Meara, trans., *The First Version of the Topography of Ireland by Giraldus Cambrensis*, Dundalk 1951.
E. Rynne, 'Toghers in Littleton Bog, Co. Tipperary', *North Munster Antiquarian Journal*, vol. IX (1965).

Chapter 3

BIBLIOGRAPHY

M. Bloch, *Feudal Society*, London 1961.
E. Curtis, *A History of Medieval Ireland from 1086 to 1513*, 2nd ed., London 1938.
F. R. H. du Boubay, *An Age of Ambition: English Society in the late Middle Ages*, London 1970.

R. Flower, *The Irish Tradition*, London 1966.
A. S. Green, *The Making of Ireland and its Undoing*, Dublin 1919.
G. A. Hayes-McCoy, *Irish Battles*, London 1969.
G. H. Orpen, *Ireland under the Normans, 1169–1216*, 4 vols, London 1911–20.
A. J. Otway-Ruthven, *A History of Medieval Ireland*, London 1968.

Chapter 4

BIBLIOGRAPHY

Anon, *Post chaise Companion*, Dublin 1784.
J. Barrow, *A Tour round Ireland*, Dublin 1836.
J. Carr, *The Stranger in Ireland*, London 1805.
Cork almanack, 1823.
T. K. Cromwell, *Excursions through Ireland (1820–21)*, London 1820.
Diary of a Tour in Ireland, 1837, National Library of Ireland MS. 194.
G. Du Noyer, *Journal of his travels in Ireland*, 1839, National Library of Ireland MS. 1441.
G. Faulkner, publisher, *Faulkner's Dublin Journal*, A volume made up of 66 numbers of the years 1807, 1808 & 1813, Dublin.
J. Gamble, *View of Society and Manners in the North of Ireland 1812*, London 1813.
J. Gough, *A Tour in Ireland in 1813 and 1814*, Dublin 1817.
J. Grant, *Impressions of Ireland and the Irish*, London 1844.
R. Colt Hoare, *Journal of a Tour in Ireland*, London 1807.
A. W. Hutton, *Technical Education as Applied to Coachbuilders and the History of Coachbuilding in Ireland*, Belfast 1902.
Irish Farmer's and Gardener's Magazine, Dublin 1834.
Irish Tourist's Illustrated Handbook for Visitors to Ireland in 1852, London 1852.
J. G. Kohl, *Ireland*, London 1843.
P. Livingstone, *The Fermanagh Story*, Enniskillen 1969.
T. McTear, 'Personal Recollections of the Beginning of the Century', *Ulster Journal of Archaeology*, 2nd series, vols 1898–99.
G. A. Montgomery, *Posting and Turnpikes*, 1826, National Library of Ireland MS. 1432.
C. Otway, *Sketches in Ireland*, Dublin 1827.
Parliamentary gazetteer of Ireland, London and Edinburgh 1846.
J. Stevenson, ed. and trans., *A Frenchman's Walk through Ireland, 1796–97*, Belfast and Dublin 1917.
G. Taylor, and A. Skinner, *Maps of the Roads in Ireland*, Dublin 1778.
W. M. Thackeray, *The Irish Sktech Book*, London 1842.
E. Wakefield, *Account of Ireland, statistical and political*, London 1812.
J. E. Walsh, *Ireland Ninety Years Ago*, Dublin 1876.
S. Watson, *Gentleman's and Citizen's Almanack*, Dublin 1780.

Chapter 5

BIBLIOGRAPHY

V. T. H. Delany, 'History of the Development of the River Shannon Navigation', *Journal of Transport History,* vol. III, no. 4, (1958), 185–94.

V. T. H. & D. R. Delany, *The Canals of the South of Ireland,* Newton Abbot, 1966.

P. J. Flanagan, 'The Ballinamore & Ballyconnell Canal', *Breifne,* vol. 3, no. 11, 347–86, and vol. 3, no. 12, 492–527.

W. A. McCutcheon, 'The Lagan Navigation', *Irish Geography,* vol. IV, no. 4, (1962), 244–55.

—— 'The Newry Navigation', *Geographical Journal,* vol. 129, pt. 4 (1963), 466–80.

—— *The Canals of the North of Ireland,* Newton Abbot, 1965.

—— 'Inland Navigations of the North of Ireland', *Technology & Culture* (U.S.A.), vol. VI, no. 4, (1965), 596–620.

D. B. McNeill, *Coastal Passenger Steamers and Inland Navigations in the North of Ireland,* Belfast, 1960.

——*Coastal Passenger Steamers and Inland Navigations in the South of Ireland,* Belfast, 1965.

M. B. Mullins, 'An Historical Sketch of Engineering in Ireland', *Trans. of the Inst. of Civil Engineers of Ireland,* vol. VI, (1859–61), 1–181.

L. T. C. Rolt, *Green and Silver,* 1949.

NOTES

1. McCutcheon, 'Inland Navigations of the North of Ireland', *Technology & Culture,* 596–620.
2. McCutcheon, 'The Newry Navigation: the earliest inland canal in the British Isles', *Geographical Journal,* vol. 129, 466–80.
3. McCutcheon, 'The Lagan Navigation', *Irish Geography,* vol. iv, 244–55.
4. W. A. McCutcheon, *The Collieries of East Tyrone,* unpublished thesis (M.A. 1958) in the Library of the Queen's University, Belfast.
5. P. J. Flanagan, 'The Ballinamore & Ballyconnell Canal', *Breifne,* vol. 3 no. 11, 347–86 and vol. 3, no. 12, 492–527.
6. McCutcheon, *The Canals of the North of Ireland.*
7. Delany, *The Canals of the South of Ireland.*
8. Sir John Carr, *The Stranger in Ireland . . . in the Year 1805,* London 1806.
9. *Second Report of the Commissioners appointed to consider & recommend a general system of Railways for Ireland,* H.C. 1837–8 (145) XXXV, 449.
10. Mr. and Mrs S. C. Hall, *Ireland: its Scenery, Character etc,* 3 vols., London 1841–43; vol. III, 275.

11. V. T. H. Delany, 'A History of the Development of the River Shannon Navigation', *Journal of Transport History*, vol. III, no. 4, (1958), 185–94.
12. J. G. Kohl, *Travels in Ireland*, London 1844.

Chapter 6

BIBLIOGRAPHY

M. O'C. Bianconi and S. J. Watson, *Bianconi, King of the Irish Roads*, Dublin 1962.
First and Second Reports of Commissioners on Railways (Parliamentary papers, 1837 vol. XXXIII, 1837–8 vol. XXXV).
T. W. Freeman, *Prefamine Ireland*, Manchester 1957.
Constantia Maxwell, *The Stranger in Ireland*, London 1854.
Mrs Morgan J. O'Connell, *Charles Bianconi*, London 1878.

Chapters 7 and 8

BIBLIOGRAPHY

J. C. Conroy, *A History of Railways in Ireland*, London 1928.
P. J. Flanagan, *The Cavan & Leitrim Railway*, London 1966.
Joseph Lee, 'The Railways in the Irish Economy', in *The Formation of the Irish Economy*, ed. L. M. Cullen, Cork 1969.
W. A. McCutcheon, *Railway History in Pictures: Ireland*, vol. I, Newton Abbot 1969.
K. A. Murray, *The Great Northern Railway (Ireland), Past, Present and Future*, Dublin 1944.
E. M. Patterson, *The Great Northern Railway of Ireland*, Newton Abbot 1962.
E. M. Patterson, *The County Donegal Railways*, Newton Abbot 1962.
K. B. Nowlan, 'Communications', in *Ulster since 1800*, eds., T. W. Moody & J. C. Beckett, Second Series, B.B.C. 1957.

Chapter 10

BIBLIOGRAPHY

J. Blackwell, 'Transport in the Developing Economy of Ireland', *The Economic and Social Research Institute*, Dublin (1969).
Committee on Industrial Organisation, *Report on the Motor Vehicle Assembly Industry*, S.O., Dublin 1962, Pr. 6728.

J. C. Conroy, *A History of Railways in Ireland,* London 1928.
W. P. Coyne (ed.), *Ireland: Industrial and Agricultural,* Dublin 1901.
The Dublin Civic Survey, Report prepared by H. T. O'Rourke and the Dublin Civic Survey Committee, Liverpool 1925.
P. Flanagan, *Transport in Ireland 1880–1910,* Dublin 1969.
P. Flanagan and C. B. Mac an tSaoir, *Dublin's Buses,* Dublin 1968.
H. Ford and S. Crowther, *Today and Tomorrow,* London 1926.
C. H. D. Howard, 'The Man on a Tricycle', in *Irish Historical Studies,* XIV, (1964–65).
Inquiry into Internal Transport, S.O., Dublin 1957, Pr. 4091.
Irish Motor Annual, 1911.
C. Jarrott, *Ten Years of Motors and Motor Racing, 1896–1906,* London 4th ed. 1956.
C. H. Lee, *Regional Economic Growth in the United Kingdom since the 1880s,* 1971.
W. A. McMaster, *A History of Motorsport in Ireland 1903–1969,* Belfast 1970.
Sir H. Osborne Mance, *The Road and Rail Transport Problem,* London 1941.
G. Maxcy and A. Silbertson, *The Motor Industry,* London 1959.
J. Meenan, *The Irish Economy since 1922,* Liverpool 1970.
R. G. Morton, *Standard Gauge Railways in the North of Ireland,* Belfast 1962.
K. Murray, *The Great Northern Railway (Ireland), Past, Present and Future,* Dublin 1944.
A. C. Pemberton, 'The Complete Cyclist', *The Isthmian Library,* vol. 2, London 1897.
Report from the Joint Select Committee on Road and Rail Transport in Northern Ireland, (Cmd. 472), Belfast 1939.
Report of Tribunal on Public Transport, S.O., Dublin 1939, Pr. 4866.
D. J. Reynolds, 'Inland Transport in Ireland: A factual survey', *Economic and Social Research Institute,* paper 10, (1962).
D. J. Reynolds, 'Road Transport: The Problems and Prospects in Ireland', *Economic and Social Research Institute,* (1963).
S. B. Saul, 'The Motor Industry in Britain in 1914', *Business History,* (Dec. 1962).
G. Turner, *The Car Makers,* London 1963.
E. White, 'The motor car arrives: a brief history of the emergent years', in *Hepolite Bulletin,* vol. 17, no. 5 (Oct. 1962), 9–15.
J. Woodford, *The Story of the Bicycle,* London 1970.

NOTES

1. As early as 1900 Guinness' were experimenting with a 15 cwt. Daimler-type lorry. *Guinness MSS.* 14 May 1900. The firm did not use motors for haulage generally until the 1920s.
2. Until 1914 the railway companies presented an image of success. The climate of optimism was represented in their expansionist plans, their diversification of activity and high dividends paid on ordinary shares. Murray, *The Great Northern Railway,* 72–81 *passim.* Meenan, *The Irish Economy since 1922,* 159.

3. White, 'The motor car arrives', *Hepolite Bulletin*, 13.
4. Riordan, *Modern Irish Trade and Industry*, London 1920, 216, 224.
5. Murray, *The Great Northern Railway*, 81.
6. Meenan, *The Irish Economy since 1922*, 158–9.
7. The greatest number of horses in Ireland (630,287) was recorded in 1895.
8. Jarrott, *Ten Years of Motors and Motor Racing 1896–1906*, 183.
9. Motor passenger services were first provided (in Belfast) in 1904 and were immediately successful. Flanagan, *Transport in Ireland 1880–1910*, 11.
10. Flanagan and Mac an tSaoir, *Dublin's Buses*, 7.
11. From 1883 when the Tramways and Public Companies (Ireland) Act was passed the government encouraged the building of light railways, tramways and standard gauge lines in remote regions. The principal means were grants and guarantees which made the ratepayers in the appropriate baronies responsible for paying interest on the shares, should the undertakings prove unprofitable. Murray, *The Great Northern Railway*, 72.
12. 'It was pleasant to be young in the age of Dunlop when so many rode out on the stale air through the fresh air of the suburbs—to the Beyond', Austin Clarke, *A Penny in the Clouds*, London 1968.
13. Howard, 'The Man on a Tricycle', *Irish Historical Studies*, 255.
14. McMaster, *A History of Motorsport in Ireland 1903–1969*, 6–7.
15. *Thom's Directory* lists bicycle agents in Dublin in 1890; by 1903 there were 52.
16. Ford, *Today and Tomorrow*, 257. He boasted 'Our Irish plant is all Irish'.
17. The B.B.C. documentary film on the life of Harry Ferguson is a good source. A copy will shortly be available at the Ulster Museum, which also has a film on J. B. Dunlop's activities in Belfast in the 1880s.
18. Lee, *Regional economic growth in the United Kingdom since the 1880s*, 88.
19. Riordan, *Modern Irish Trade and Industry*, 102.
20. Other early Irish bicycle manufacturers were: the City Cycle Co. of Dublin, who advertised as sole makers of the 'Emerald Isle' which they described as Ireland's best bicycle; the Raleigh Cycle Co.; W. J. Chambers of Belfast, makers of 'Prospect cycles and motors'; Bernard Harrell of Belfast, maker of the Ulster Eagle cycle: *Irish Directory*, 1909.
21. C.I.O. *Report on the Motor Vehicle Assembly Industry*, 100–101. This report is critical of the contribution made by this industry to Irish economic growth despite the fact that it gave employment to almost 5,000 people in 1959.
22. There were 46,000 miles of road in the 26 counties, of which 4,000 miles were main roads. Conroy, *A History of Railways in Ireland*, 369.
23. Coyne, *Ireland: Industrial and Agricultural*, 23.
24. Reynolds, 'Inland Transport in Ireland: A Factual Survey', *E. S. R. I.*, 1.
25. In 1959–60 expenditure on roads was less than half of the taxation levied on motor vehicles and their use in the year 1959–60. *Ibid.*, 4.
26. McCutcheon, *Canals of the North of Ireland*, 16.

27. Between 1894 and 1904 free grants of £1,394,000 were made to improve transit facilities. Conroy, *A History of Railways in Ireland*, 184.
28. The total capital of the Irish railway system was almost £47 million in 1921. Meenan, *The Irish Economy since 1922*.
29. Numbers of private cars in the twenty-six counties increased from 52,200 in 1947 to 135,000 in 1957 and to 314,400 in 1967. Blackwell, 'Transport in the Developing Economy of Ireland', *E.S.R.I.*, 2.

Chapter 11

BIBLIOGRAPHY

J. P. Beddy, *Report of Committee of Enquiry in Internal Transport*, 1957.
C.I.E. Annual Reports, 1950–1 and 1951–2.
C.I.E. Report on Internal Public Transport, 1963.
J. C. Conroy, *A History of the Railways in Ireland*, London 1928.
Department of Local Government: Report on Standards for the Classification and Layout of Roads, 1944.
James Gorman, 'The Irish Air Companies' in *Administration*, vol. 3, no. 4, (1955).
J. Milne, *Report on Transport in Ireland*, 1940.
P. O'Keefe, 'Economic Aspects of Road Improvement in Ireland' in *Administration*, vol. X, (1962), 139–76.
Public Road Freight Transport in Northern Ireland, (1956), Cmd. 361.
Report of Tribunal of Enquiry on Public Transport, 1939.
D. J. Reynolds, 'Inland Transport in Ireland: A Factual Survey', *Economic and Social Research Institute*, paper no. 13.
Ulster Yearbook 1963–65, 1971.